Beneath Apple DOS

Eighth printing, November 1985

By Don Worth and Pieter Lechner

A product of

QUALITY SOFTWARE
21601 Marilla Street
Chatsworth, CA 91311

ISBN 0-912985-00-3

DISCLAIMER

Quality Software shall have no liability or responsibility to the purchaser or any other person or entity with respect to any liability, loss or damage caused or alleged to be caused directly or indirectly by this manual or its use, including but not limited to any interruption in service, loss of business and anticipatory profits or consequential damages resulting from the use of this product.

TABLE OF CONTENTS

TABLE OF CONTENTS

ACKNOWLEDGEMENTS

Thanks go to Vic Tolomei for his assistance in dissecting DOS 3.1 and to Lou Rivas for his patient proofreading. Thanks also to my wife Carley for putting up with the clackety clack of my Diablo long into the night.

Don D. Worth

Thanks to the people at Computerland of South Bay (California) who lent me support both of their time and equipment, and special thanks to John Gottuso, whose encouragement helped me to complete the task.

Pieter M. Lechner

CHAPTER 1
INTRODUCTION

Beneath Apple DOS is intended to serve as a companion to Apple's DOS Manual, providing additional information for the advanced programmer or the novice Apple user who wants to know more about the structure of diskettes. It is not the intent of this manual to replace the documentation provided by Apple Computer Inc. Although, for the sake of continuity, some of the material covered in the Apple manual is also covered here, it will be assumed that the reader is reasonably familiar with the contents of the DOS Manual. Since all chapters presented here may not be of use to each Apple owner, each has been written to stand on its own.

The information presented here is a result of intensive disassembly and annotation of various versions of DOS by the authors and by other experienced systems programmers. It also draws from application notes, articles, and discussions with knowledgeable people. This manual was not prepared with the assistance of Apple Computer Inc. Although no guarantee can be made concerning the accuracy of the information presented here, all of the material included in Beneath Apple DOS has been thoroughly researched and tested.

There were several reasons for writing Beneath Apple DOS:

To show direct assembly language access to DOS.
To help you to fix clobbered diskettes.
To correct errors and omissions in the Apple documentation.
To allow you to customize DOS to fit your needs.
To provide complete information on diskette formatting.

THERE WERE SEVERAL REASONS FOR WRITING "BENEATH APPLE DOS".....

When Apple Computer Inc. introduced its Disk Operating System (DOS) version 3 in 1978 to support the new DISK II drive, very little documentation was provided. Later, when DOS 3.2 was released, a 178 page instructional and reference manual became available covering the use of DOS from BASIC in depth and even touched upon some of the internal workings of DOS. With the advent of DOS 3.3, the old 3.2 manual was updated but the body of information in it remained essentially intact. Beyond these Apple manuals, there have been no significant additions to the documentation on DOS, apart from a few articles in APPLE user group magazines and newsletters. This manual takes up where the Disk Operating System Manual leaves off.

Throughout this manual, discussion centers primarily on DOS version 3.3. The reasons for this are that 3.3 was the most recent release of DOS at the time of this writing and that it differs less from DOS 3.2 than one would imagine. Wherever there is a major difference between the various DOS releases in a given topic, each release will be covered.

In addition to the DOS dependent information provided, many of the discussions also apply to other operating systems on the Apple II and Apple III. For example, disk formatting at the track and sector level is, for the most part, the same.

CHAPTER 2
THE EVOLUTION OF DOS

Since its introduction, Apple DOS has gone through three major versions. All of these versions look very much the same on the surface. All commands supported by DOS 3.3 are also supported in 3.2 and 3.1. The need for additional versions has been more to fix errors in DOS and to make minor enhancements than to provide additional functionality. Only DOS 3.3 has offered any major improvement in function; an increase in the number of sectors that will fit on a track from 13 to 16.

DOS 3 - 29 June 1978
DOS 3.1 - 20 July 1978

The first release of DOS was apparently a victim of a rush at Apple to introduce the DISK II. As such, it had a number of bugs. With the movement towards the APPLE II PLUS and the introduction of the AUTOSTART ROM, a new release was needed.

DOS 3.2 - 16 February 1979

Although DOS 3.2 embodied more changes from its predecessor than any other release of DOS, 90% of the basic structure of DOS 3.1 was retained. The major differences between DOS 3.1 and 3.2 and later versions of DOS are listed below:

- NOMON C,I,O is the initial default under DOS 3.2. MON C,I,O was the default under DOS 3.1.
- Input prompts (>,],*) are echoed when MON O is in effect, not under MON I as was the case under 3.1.
- When a DOS command was entered from the keyboard, DOS executed it and then passed a blank followed by a carriage return to BASIC under 3.1. Under 3.2 only a carriage return is passed.
- Under 3.2, certain commands may not be entered from the keyboard but may only be used within a BASIC program (READ, WRITE, POSITION, OPEN, APPEND).
- Under 3.2, when LOADing an APPLESOFT program, DOS automatically converts from APPLESOFT ROM format to APPLESOFT RAM format if the RAM version of BASIC is in use and vice versa.
- DOS 3.1 could not read lower case characters from a text file; DOS 3.2 can.

THE EVOLUTION OF APPLE DOS.

- Some DOS commands are allowed to create a new file, others will not. Under DOS 3.1, any reference to a file that didn't exist, caused it to be created. This forced DOS 3.1 to then delete it if a new file was not desired. (LOAD XYZ under 3.1 if XYZ did not exist, created XYZ, deleted XYZ, and then printed the file not found error message.) Under 3.2, OPEN is allowed to create a file if one does not exist, but LOAD may not.
- Under 3.1, exiting to the monitor required that the monitor status register location ($48) be set to zero before reentering DOS. Under DOS 3.2 this is no longer necessary.
- The Read/Write-Track/Sector (RWTS) section of DOS disables interrupts while it is executing. Under 3.1, RWTS could be interrupted by a peripheral while writing to a disk, destroying the disk.
- The default for the B (byte offset) keyword is 0 under 3.2.
- DOS was reassembled for 3.2 causing most of its interesting locations and routines to move slightly. This played havoc with user programs and utilities which had DOS addresses built into them.
- Additional file types (beyond T, I, A, and B) are defined within DOS 3.2, although no commands yet support them. The new types are S, R, a new A, and a new B. R has subsequently been used by the DOS TOOLKIT for relocatable object module assembler files. At present, no other use is made of these extra file types.
- Support was added under 3.2 for the AUTOSTART ROM.
- All files open when a disk full condition occurs are closed by DOS 3.2.
- As with each new release of DOS, several new programs were added to the master diskette for 3.2. Among these was UPDATE 3.2, a replacement for MASTER CREATE, the utility for creating master diskettes. UPDATE 3.2 converts a slave into a master and allows the HELLO file to be renamed.

DOS 3.2.1 - 31 July 1979

DOS 3.2.1 was essentially a "maintenance release" of DOS 3.2. Minor patches were made to RWTS and the COPY program to correct a timing problem when a dual drive copy was done. Additional delays were added following a switch between drives.

DOS 3.3 - 25 August 1980

Introduced in mid 1980 as a hardware/software upgrade from DOS 3.2.1, the DOS 3.3 package includes new bootstrap and state ROM chips for the disk controller card which provide the capability to format, read, and write a diskette with 16 sectors. (These ROMs are the same ones used with the LANGUAGE SYSTEM.) This improvement represents almost a 25% increase in available disk space over the old 13 sector format. Also included in the 3.3 package is an updated version of the DOS manual, a BASICS diskette (for 13 sector boots), and a master diskette. Although the RWTS portion of DOS was almost totally rewritten, the rest of DOS was not reassembled and only received a few patches:

- The initial DOS bootstrap loader was moved to $800 under 3.3. It was at $300 under 3.2. In addition, as stored on the diskette (track 0 sector 0) it is nibbilized in the same way as all other sectors under 3.3.
- A bug in APPEND which caused it to position improperly if the file was a multiple of 256 bytes long was fixed under 3.3.
- A VERIFY command is internally executed after every SAVE or BSAVE under 3.3.
- All 4 bytes are used in the Volume Table Of Contents (VTOC) free sector bit map when keeping track of free sectors. This allows DOS to handle up to 32 sectors per track. Of course, RWTS will only handle 16 sectors due to hardware limitations.
- If a LANGUAGE CARD is present, DOS stores a zero on it at $E000 during bootstrap to force the HELLO program on the master diskette to reload BASIC.
- DOS is read into memory from the top down (backwards) under 3.3 rather than the bottom up. Its image is still stored in the same order on the diskette (tracks 0, 1, and 2), however.
- Additional programs added to the master diskette under 3.3 include FID, a generalized file utility which allows individual files or groups of files to be copied, MUFFIN, a conversion copy routine to allow 3.2 files to be moved to 16 sector 3.3 diskettes, BOOT 13, a program which will boot a 13 sector diskette, and a new COPY program which will also support single drive copies.
- Under 3.2, speed differences in some drives prevented their use together with the DOS COPY program. Because the COPY program was rewritten under 3.3, that restriction no longer applies.

DOS 3.3 - 1 January 1983

This "maintenance release" of DOS was introduced with the Apple IIe computer. It contains a few minor patches and no additional function.

- A patch was introduced in DOS 3.3 to fix a bug in APPEND processing. This patch also had bugs. Additional patches were added to (hopefully) correct this problem.
- An error in the POSITION calculation for large files is corrected in this release.
- A few instructions were added to properly support the 80 column display on the Apple IIe.
- The system master diskette contains some different files. Notably, a fast loader for the language card and all of the example programs have been moved to a separate diskette.

CHAPTER 3
DISKETTE FORMATTING

Apple Computer's excellent manual on the Disk Operating System (DOS) provides only very basic information about how diskettes are formatted. This chapter will explain in detail how information is structured on a diskette. The first section will contain a brief introduction to the hardware, and may be skipped by those already familiar with the DOS manual.

TRACKS AND SECTORS

For system housekeeping, DOS divides diskettes into tracks and sectors. This is done during the initialization process. A track is a physically defined circular path which is concentric with the hole in the center of the diskette. Each track is identified by its distance from the center of the disk. Similar to a phonograph stylus, the read/write head of the disk drive may be positioned over any given track. The tracks are similar to the grooves in a record, but they are not connected in a spiral. Much like playing a record, the diskette is spun at a constant speed while the data is read from or written to its surface with the read/write head. Apple formats its diskettes into 35 tracks. They are numbered from 0 to 34, track 0 being the outermost track and track 34 the innermost. Figure 3.1 illustrates the concept of tracks, although they are invisible to the eye on a real diskette.

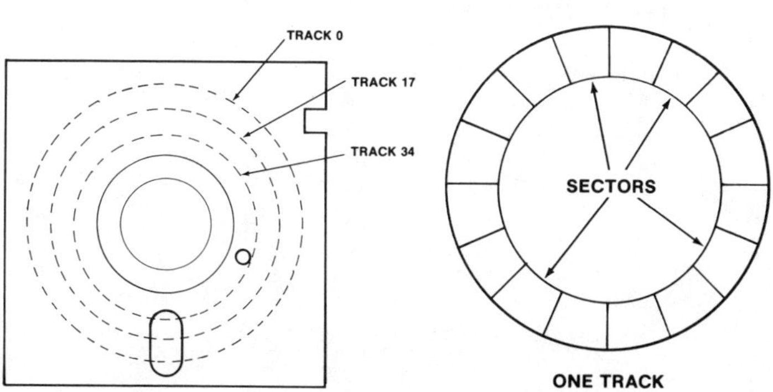

FIGURE 3.1

It should be pointed out, for the sake of accuracy, that the disk arm can position itself over 70 "phases". To move the arm past one track to the next, two phases of the stepper motor, which moves the arm, must be cycled. This implies that data might be stored on 70 tracks, rather than 35. Unfortunately, the resolution of the read/write head and the accuracy of the stepper motor are such, that attempts to use these phantom "half" tracks create so much cross-talk that data is lost or overwritten. Although the standard DOS uses only even phases, some protected disks use odd phases or combinations of the two, provided that no two tracks are closer than two phases from one another. See APPENDIX B for more information on protection schemes.

A sector is a subdivision of a track. It is the smallest unit of "updatable" data on the diskette. DOS generally reads or writes data a sector at a time. This is to avoid using a large chunk of memory as a buffer to read or write an entire track. Apple DOS has used two different track formats--one divides the track into 13 sectors, the other into 16 sectors. The sectoring does not use the index hole, provided on most diskettes, to locate the first sector of the track. The implication is that the software must be able to locate any given track and sector with no help from the hardware. This scheme, known as "soft sectoring", takes a little more space for storage but allows flexibility, as evidenced by the change from 13 sectors to the present 16 sectors per track. Figure 3.2 categorizes the amount of data stored on a diskette under both 13 and 16 sector formats.

DISK ORGANIZATION

```
TRACKS
  All DOS versions................35

SECTORS PER TRACK
  DOS 3.2.1 and earlier...........13
  DOS 3.3.........................16

SECTORS PER DISKETTE
  DOS 3.2.1 and earlier..........455
  DOS 3.3........................560

BYTES PER SECTOR
  All DOS versions...............256

BYTES PER DISKETTE
  DOS 3.2.1 and earlier.......116480
  DOS 3.3.....................143360

USABLE* SECTORS FOR DATA STORAGE
  DOS 3.2.1 and earlier..........403
  DOS 3.3........................496

USABLE* BYTES PER DISKETTE
  DOS 3.2.1 and earlier.......103168
  DOS 3.3.....................126976

* Excludes DOS, VTOC, and CATALOG
```

FIGURE 3.2

TRACK FORMATTING

Up to this point we have broken down the structure of data to the track and sector level. To better understand how data is stored and retrieved, we will start at the bottom and work up.

As this manual is primarily concerned with software, no attempt will be made to deal with the specifics of the hardware. For example, while in fact data is stored as a continuous stream of analog signals, we will deal with discrete digital data, i.e. a 0 or a 1. We recognize that the hardware converts analog data to digital data but how this is accomplished is beyond the scope of this manual.

Data bits are recorded on the diskette in precise intervals. The hardware recognizes each of these intervals as either a Ø or a 1. We will define these intervals to be "bit cells". A bit cell can be thought of as the distance the diskette moves in four machine cycles, which is about four microseconds. Using this representation, data written to and read back from the diskette takes the form shown in Figure 3.3. The data pattern shown represents a binary value of 1Ø1.

BITS ON DISK

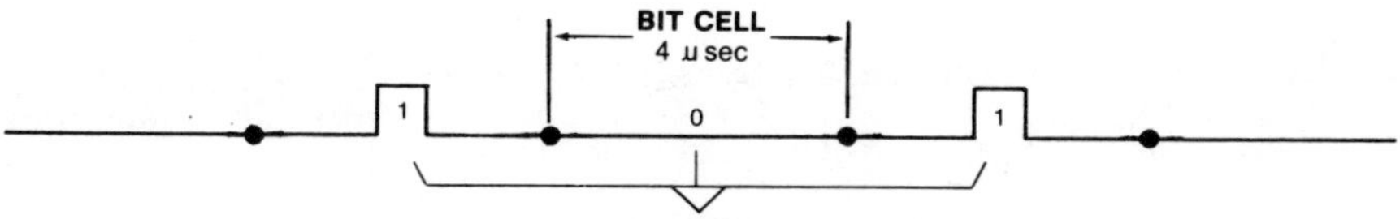

FIGURE 3.3

A byte as recorded on the disk consists of eight (8) consecutive bit cells. The most significant bit cell is usually referred to as bit cell 7 and the least significant bit cell as bit cell 0. When reference is made to a specific data bit (i.e. data bit 5), it is with respect to the corresponding bit cell (bit cell 5). Data is written and read serially, one bit at a time. Thus, during a write operation, bit cell 7 of each byte is written first, with bit cell 0 written last. Correspondingly, when data is being read back from the diskette, bit cell 7 is read first and bit cell 0 is read last. Figure 3.4 illustrates the relationship of the bits within a byte.

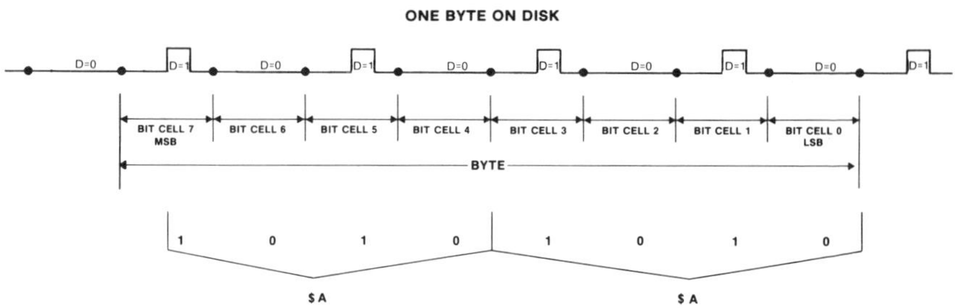

FIGURE 3.4

To graphically show how bits are stored and retrieved, we must take certain liberties. The diagrams are a representation of what functionally occurs within the disk drive. For the purposes of our presentation, the hardware interface to the diskette will be represented as an eight bit "data latch". While the hardware involves considerably more complication, from a software standpoint it is reasonable to use the data latch, as it accurately embodies the function of data flow to and from the diskette.

Figure 3.5 shows the three bits, 101, being read from the diskette data stream into the data latch. Of course another five bits would be read to fill the latch.

Writing data can be depicted in much the same way (see Figure 3.6). It should be noted that, while in write mode, zeros are being brought into the data latch to replace the data being written. It is the task of the software to make sure that the latch is loaded and instructed to write in 32 cycle intervals. If not, zero bits will continue to be written every four cycles, which is, in fact, exactly how self-sync bytes are created. Self sync bytes will be covered in detail shortly.

READING DATA FROM DISKETTE

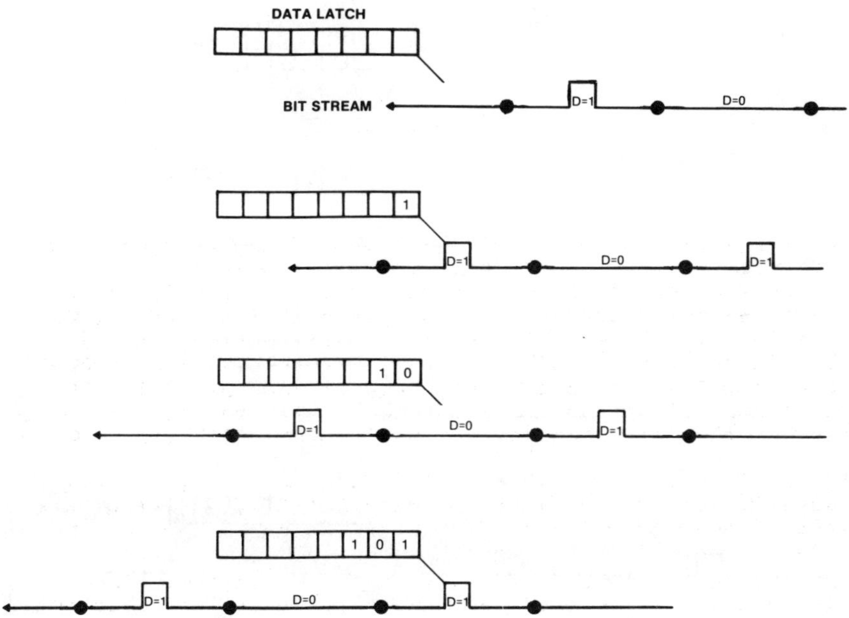

FIGURE 3.5

WRITING DATA TO DISKETTE

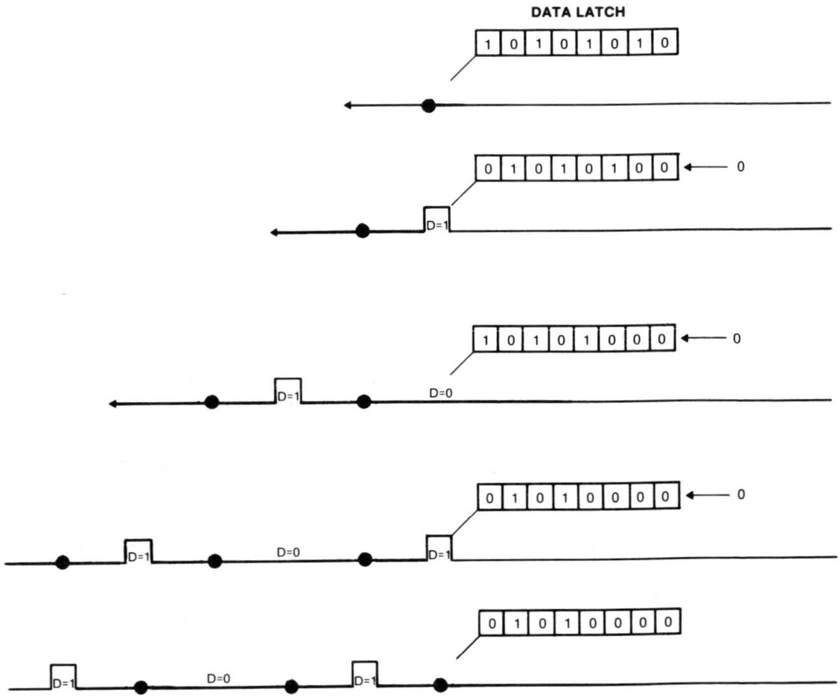

FIGURE 3.6

A "field" is made up of a group of consecutive bytes. The number of bytes varies, depending upon the nature of the field. The two types of fields present on a diskette are the Address Field and the Data Field. They are similar in that they both contain a prologue, a data area, a checksum, and an epilogue. Each field on a track is separated from adjacent fields by a number of bytes. These areas of separation are called "gaps" and are provided for two reasons. One, they allow the updating of one field without affecting adjacent fields (on the Apple, only data fields are updated). Secondly, they allow the computer time to decode the address field before the corresponding data field can pass beneath the read/write head.

All gaps are primarily alike in content, consisting of self-sync hexadecimal FF's, and vary only in the number of bytes they contain. Figure 3.7 is a diagram of a portion of a typical track, broken into its major components.

TRACK FORMAT

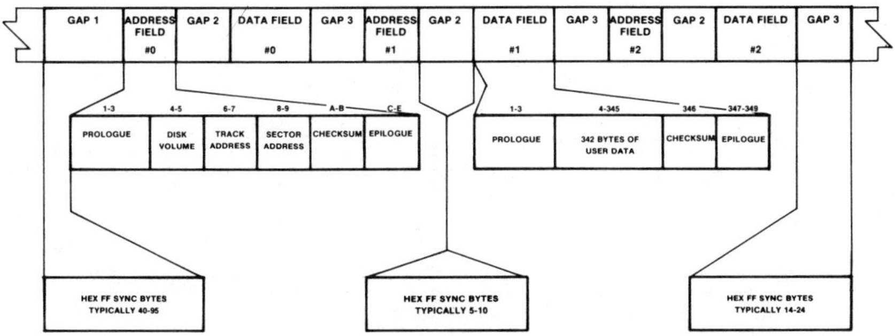

FIGURE 3.7

Self-sync or auto-sync bytes are special bytes that make up the three different types of gaps on a track. They are so named because of their ability to automatically bring the hardware into synchronization with data bytes on the disk. The difficulty in doing this lies in the fact that the hardware reads bits and the data must be stored as eight bit bytes. It has been mentioned that a track is literally a continuous stream of data bits. In fact, at the bit level, there is no way to determine where a byte starts or ends, because each bit cell is exactly the same, written in precise intervals with its neighbors. When the drive is instructed to read data, it will start wherever it happens to be on a particular track. That could be anywhere among the 50,000 or so bits on a track. The hardware finds the first bit cell with a "1" bit in it and proceeds to read it and the following seven data bits into the eight bit latch. In effect, the hardware assumes that it started at the beginning of a data byte. Of course, in reality, the odds of its having started at the beginning of a byte are less than one in four. Pictured in Figure 3.8 is a small portion of a track.

AN EXAMPLE BIT STREAM ON THE DISK

0 1 1 0 1 0 1 1 1 0 1 0 1 1 0 0 1 1 1 1 0 1 1 0 1 1 1 0 1 0 1

FIGURE 3.8

There is no way from looking at the data to tell what bytes are represented, because we don't know where to start. This is exactly the problem that self-sync bytes overcome.

A self-sync byte is defined to be a hexadecimal FF with a special difference. It is, in fact, a 10 bit byte rather than an eight bit byte. Its two extra bits are zeros. Figure 3.9 shows the difference between a normal data hex FF that might be found elsewhere on the disk and a self-sync hex FF byte.

NORMAL BYTE HEX FF

1	1	1	1	1	1	1	1

SELF-SYNC BYTE HEX FF

1	1	1	1	1	1	1	1	0	0

FIGURE 3.9

A self-sync is generated by using a 40 cycle (microsecond) loop while writing an FF. A bit is written every four cycles, so two of the zero bits brought into the data latch while the FF was being written are also written to the disk, making the 10 bit byte. (DOS 3.2.1 and earlier versions use a nine bit byte due to the hardware's inability to always detect two consecutive zero bits.) It can be shown, using Figure 3.10, that four self-sync bytes are sufficient to guarantee that the hardware is reading valid data. The reason for this is that the hardware requires the first bit of a byte to be a 1. Pictured at the top of the figure is a stream of five FFs, four self-sync FFs followed by a normal FF. Each row below that demonstrates what the hardware will read should it start reading at any given bit in the first byte. In each case, by the time the four self-sync bytes have passed beneath the read/write head, the hardware will be "synced" to read the bytes that follow. As long as the disk is left in read mode, it will continue to correctly interpret the data unless there is an error on the track.

AUTOSYNC BYTES

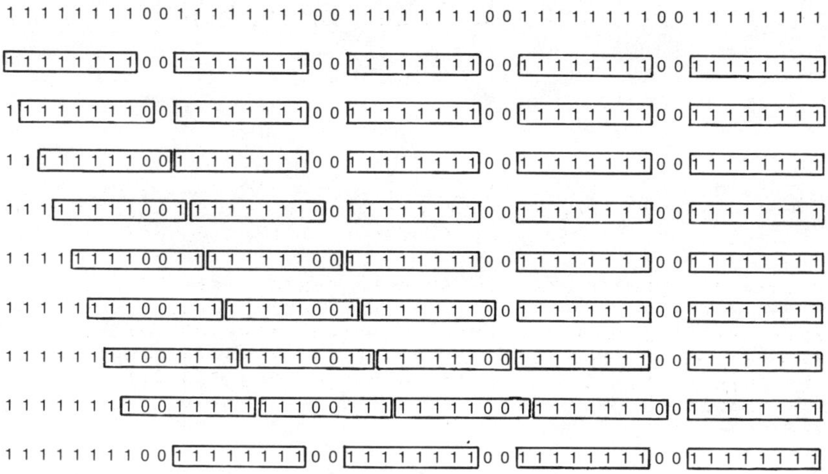

FIGURE 3.10

We can now discuss the particular portions of a track in detail. The three gaps will be covered first. Unlike some other disk formats, the size of the three gap types will vary from drive to drive and even from track to track. During the initialization process, DOS will start with large gaps and keep making them smaller until an entire track can be written without overlapping itself. DOS makes sure that each gap type (see Figure 3.7) contains a minimum of four self-sync bytes. The result is fairly uniform gap sizes within each particular track.

Gap 1 is the first data written to a track during initialization. Its purpose is twofold. The gap originally consists of 128 bytes of self-sync, a large enough area to insure that all portions of a track will contain data. Since the speed of a particular drive may vary, the total length of the track in bytes is uncertain, and the percentage occupied by data is unknown. The initialization process is set up, however, so that even on drives of differing speeds, the last data field written will overlap Gap 1, providing continuity over the entire physical track. Care is taken to make sure the remaining portion of Gap 1 is at least as long as a typical Gap 3 (in practice its length is usually more than 40 sync bytes), enabling it to serve as a Gap 3 type for Address Field number 0 (See Figure 3.7 for clarity).

Gap 2 appears after each Address Field and before each Data Field. Its length varies from five to ten bytes on a normal drive. The primary purpose of Gap 2 is to provide time for the information in an Address Field to be decoded by the computer before a read or write takes place. If the gap were too short, the beginning of the Data Field might spin past while DOS was still determining if this was the sector to be read. The 240 odd cycles that six self-sync bytes provide seems ample time to decode an address field. When a Data Field is written there is no guarantee that the write will occur in exactly the same spot each time. This is due to the fact that the drive which is rewriting the Data Field may not be the one which originally INITed or wrote it. Since the speed of the drives can vary, it is possible that the write could start in mid-byte. (See Figure 3.11) This is not a problem as long as the difference in positioning is not great. To insure the integrity of Gap 2, when writing a data field, five self-sync bytes are written prior to writing the Data Field itself. This serves two purposes. Since relatively little time is spent decoding an address field, the five bytes help place the Data Field near its

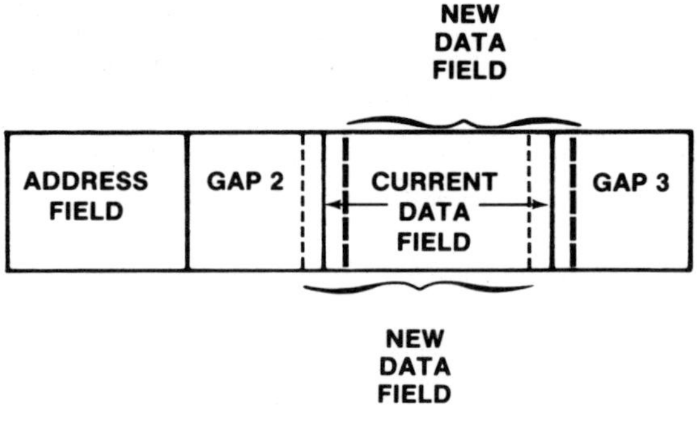

FIGURE 3.11

original position. Secondly, and more importantly, the five self-sync bytes guarantee read synchronization. It is probable that, in writing a data field, at least one sync byte will be destroyed. This is because, just as in reading bits on the track, the write may not begin on a byte boundary, thus altering an existing byte. Figure 3.12 illustrates this.

WRITING OUT OF SYNC

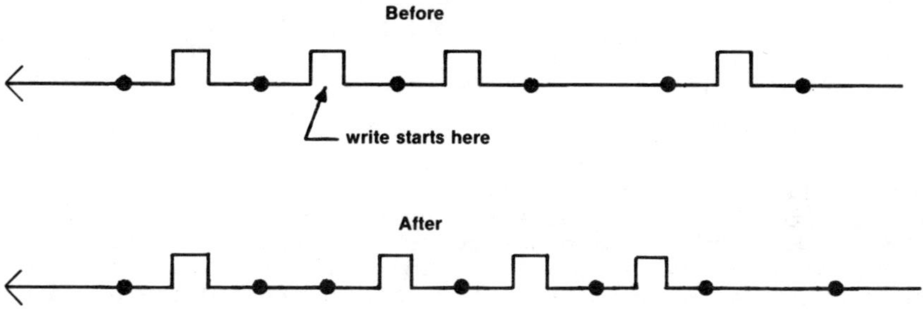

FIGURE 3.12

Gap 3 appears after each Data Field and before each Address Field. It is longer than Gap 2 and generally ranges from 14 to 24 bytes in length. It is quite similar in purpose to Gap 2. Gap 3 allows the additional time needed to manipulate the data that has been read before the next sector is to be read. The length of Gap 3 is not as critical as that of Gap 2. If the following Address Field is missed, DOS can always wait for the next time it spins around under the read/write head, at most one revolution of the disk. Since Address Fields are never rewritten, there is no problem with this gap providing synchronization, since only the first part of the gap can be overwritten or damaged. (See Figure 3.11 for clarity)

An examination of the contents of the two types of fields is in order. The Address Field contains the "address" or identifying information about the Data Field which follows it. The volume, track, and sector number of any given sector can be thought of as its "address", much like a country, city, and street number might identify a house. As shown previously in Figure 3.7, there are a number of components which make up the Address Field. A more detailed illustration is given in Figure 3.13.

ADDRESS FIELD

PROLOGUE	VOLUME	TRACK	SECTOR	CHECKSUM	EPILOGUE
D5 AA 96	XX YY	XX YY	XX YY	XX YY	DE AA EB

ODD-EVEN ENCODED

DATA BYTE — $D_7 D_6 D_5 D_4 D_3 D_2 D_1 D_0$

XX — $1\ D_7\ 1\ D_5\ 1\ D_3\ 1\ D_1$

YY — $1\ D_6\ 1\ D_4\ 1\ D_2\ 1\ D_0$

FIGURE 3.13

The prologue consists of three bytes which form a unique sequence, found in no other component of the track. This fact enables DOS to locate an Address Field with almost no possibility of error. The three bytes are $D5, $AA, and $96. The $D5 and $AA are reserved (never written as data) thus insuring the uniqueness of the prologue. The $96, following this unique string, indicates that the data following constitutes an Address Field (as opposed to a Data Field). The address information follows next, consisting of the volume, track, and sector number and a checksum. This information is absolutely essential for DOS to know where it is positioned on a particular diskette. The checksum is computed by exclusive-ORing the first three pieces of information, and is used to verify its integrity. Lastly follows the epilogue, which contains the three bytes $DE, $AA and $EB. The $EB is only partially written during initialization, and therefore is never verified when an Address Field is read. The epilogue bytes are sometimes referred to as "bit-slip marks," which provide added assurance that the drive is still in sync with the bytes on the disk. These bytes are probably unnecessary, but do provide a means of double checking.

DATA FIELD

The other field type is the Data Field. Much like the Address Field, it consists of a prologue, data, checksum, and an epilogue. (Refer to Figure 3.14) The prologue is different only in the third byte. The bytes are $D5, $AA, and $AD, which again form a unique sequence, enabling DOS to locate the beginning of the sector data. The data consists of 342 bytes of encoded data. The encoding scheme used will be discussed in the next section. The data is followed by a checksum byte, used to verify the integrity of the data just read. The epilogue portion of the Data Field is absolutely identical to the epilogue in the Address Field and it serves the same function.

DATA FIELD

FIGURE 3.14

DATA FIELD ENCODING

Due to Apple's hardware, it is not possible to read all 256 possible byte values from a diskette. This is not a great problem, but it does require that the data written to the disk be encoded. Three different techniques have been used. The first one, which is currently used in Address Fields, involves writing a data byte as two disk bytes, one containing the odd bits, and the other containing the even bits. It would thus require 512 "disk" bytes for each 256 byte sector of data. Had this technique been used for sector data, no more than 10 sectors would have fit on a track. This amounts to about 88K of data per diskette, or roughly 72K of space available to the user; typical for 5 1/4 single density drives.

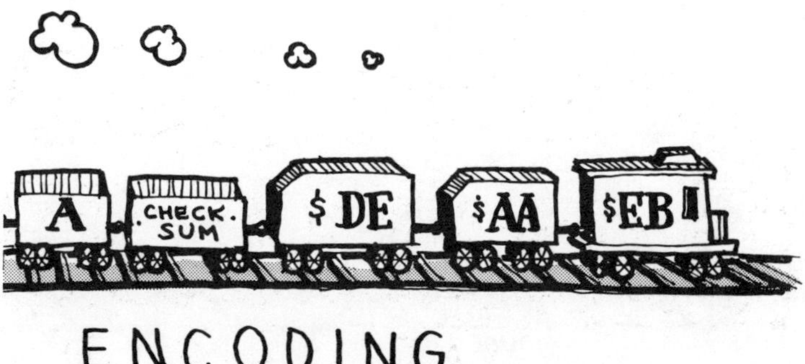

Fortunately, a second technique for writing data to diskette was devised that allows 13 sectors per track. This new method involved a "5 and 3" split of the data bits, versus the "4 and 4" mentioned earlier. Each byte written to the disk contains five valid bits rather than four. This requires 410 "disk" bytes to store a 256 byte sector. This latter density allows the now well known 13 sectors per track format used by DOS 3 through DOS 3.2.1. The "5 and 3" scheme represented a hefty 33% increase over comparable drives of the day.

Currently, of course, DOS 3.3 features 16 sectors per track and provides a 23% increase in disk storage over the 13 sector format. This was made possible by a hardware modification (the P6 PROM on the disk controller card) which allowed a "6 and 2" split of the data. The change was to the logic of the "state machine" in the P6 PROM, now allowing two consecutive zero bits in data bytes.

These three different encoding techniques will now be covered in some detail. The hardware for DOS 3.2.1 (and earlier versions of DOS) imposed a number of restrictions upon how data could be stored and retrieved. It required that a disk byte have the high bit set and, in addition, no two consecutive bits could be zero. The odd-even "4 and 4" technique meets these requirements. Each data byte is represented as two bytes, one containing the even data bits and the other the odd data bits. Figure 3.15 illustrates this transformation. It should be noted that the unused bits are all set to one to guarantee meeting the two requirements.

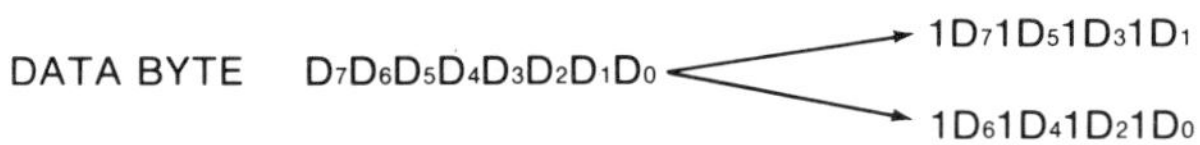

FIGURE 3.15

No matter what value the original data data byte has, this technique insures that the high bit is set and that there can not be two consecutive zero bits. The "4 and 4" technique is used to store the information (volume, track, sector, checksum) contained in the Address Field. It is quite easy to decode the data, since the byte with the odd bits is simply shifted left and logically ANDed with the byte containing the even bits. This is illustrated in Figure 3.16.

$$\begin{array}{rl} & D_7\ 1\ D_5\ 1\ D_3\ 1\ D_1\ 1 \quad \text{(shifted left)} \\ \text{AND} & \underline{1\ D_6\ 1\ D_4\ 1\ D_2\ 1\ D_0} \\ & D_7D_6D_5D_4D_3D_2D_1D_0 \end{array}$$

FIGURE 3.16

It is important that the least significant bit contain a 1 when the odd-bits byte is left shifted. The entire operation is carried out in the RDADR subroutine at $B944 in DOS (48K).

The major difficulty with the above technique is that it takes up a lot of room on the track. To overcome this deficiency the "5 and 3" encoding technique was developed. It is so named because, instead of splitting the bytes in half, as in the odd-even technique, they are split five and three. A byte would have the form 000XXXXX, where X is a valid data bit. The above byte could range in value from $00 to $1F, a total of 32 different values. It so happens that there are 34 valid "disk" bytes, ranging from $AA up to $FF, which meet the two requirements (high bit set, no consecutive zero bits). Two bytes, $D5 and $AA, were chosen as reserved bytes, thus leaving an exact mapping between five bit data bytes and eight bit "disk" bytes. The process of converting eight bit data bytes to eight bit "disk" bytes, then, is twofold. An overview is diagrammed in Figure 3.17.

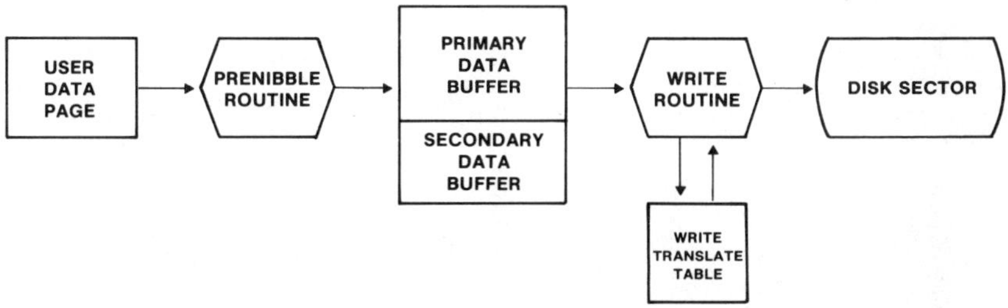

FIGURE 3.17

First, the 256 bytes that will make up a sector must be translated to five bit bytes. This is done by the "prenibble" routine at $B800. It is a fairly involved process, involving a good deal of bit rearrangement. Figure 3.18 shows the before and after of prenibbilizing. On the left is a buffer of eight bit data bytes, as passed to the RWTS subroutine package by DOS. Each byte in this buffer is represented by a letter (A, B, C, etc.) and each bit by a number (7 through 0). On the right side are the results of the transformation. The primary buffer contains five distinct areas of five bit bytes (the top three bits of the eight bit bytes zero-filled) and the secondary buffer contains three areas, graphically illustrating the name "5 and 3".

"5 and 3" PRENIBBILIZING

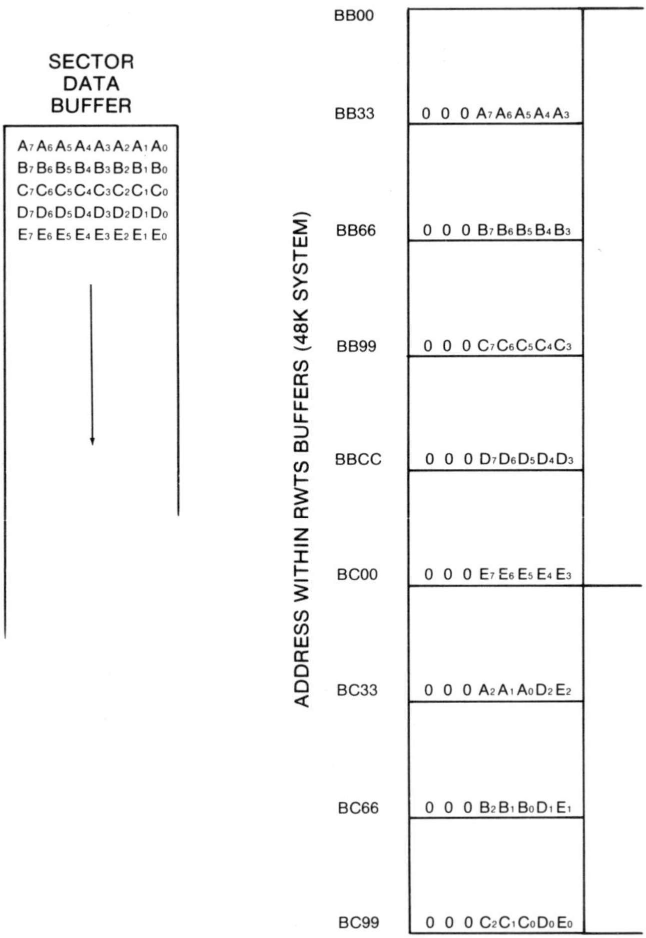

FIGURE 3.18

A total of 410 bytes are needed to store the original 256. This can be calculated by finding the total bits of data (256 x 8 = 2048) and dividing that by the number of bits per byte (2048 / 5 = 409.6). (two bits are not used) Once this process is completed, the data is further transformed to make it valid "disk" bytes, meeting the disk's requirements. This is much easier, involving a one to one look-up in the table given in Figure 3.19.

"5 and 3"
WRITE TRANSLATE TABLE

00 = AB	10 = DD
01 = AD	11 = DE
02 = AE	12 = DF
03 = AF	13 = EA
04 = B5	14 = EB
05 = B6	15 = ED
06 = B7	16 = EE
07 = BA	17 = EF
08 = BB	18 = F5
09 = BD	19 = F6
0A = BE	1A = F7
0B = BF	1B = FA
0C = D6	1C = FB
0D = D7	1D = FD
0E = DA	1E = FE
0F = DB	1F = FF

AA, D5 } Reserved Bytes

FIGURE 3.19

The Data Field has a checksum much like the one in the Address Field, used to verify the integrity of the data. It also involves exclusive-ORing the information, but, due to time constraints during reading bytes, it is implemented differently. The data is exclusive-ORed in pairs before being transformed by the look-up table in Figure 3.19. This can best be illustrated by Figure 3.20 on the following page.*

The reason for this transformation can be better understood by examining how the information is retrieved from the disk. The read routine must read a byte, transform it, and store it -- all in under 32 cycles (the time taken to write a byte) or the information will be lost. By using the checksum computation to decode data, the transformation shown in Figure 3.20 greatly facilitates the time constraint. As the data is being read from a sector the accumulator contains the cumulative result of all previous bytes, exclusive-ORed together. The value of the accumulator after any exclusive-OR operation is the actual data byte for that point in the series. This process is diagrammed in Figure 3.21.*

*Figures 3.20 and 3.21 present the nibblizing process used by the "6 and 2" encoding technique. However, the concept is the same for the "5 and 3" technique.

WRITING TO DISKETTE, DOS 3.3

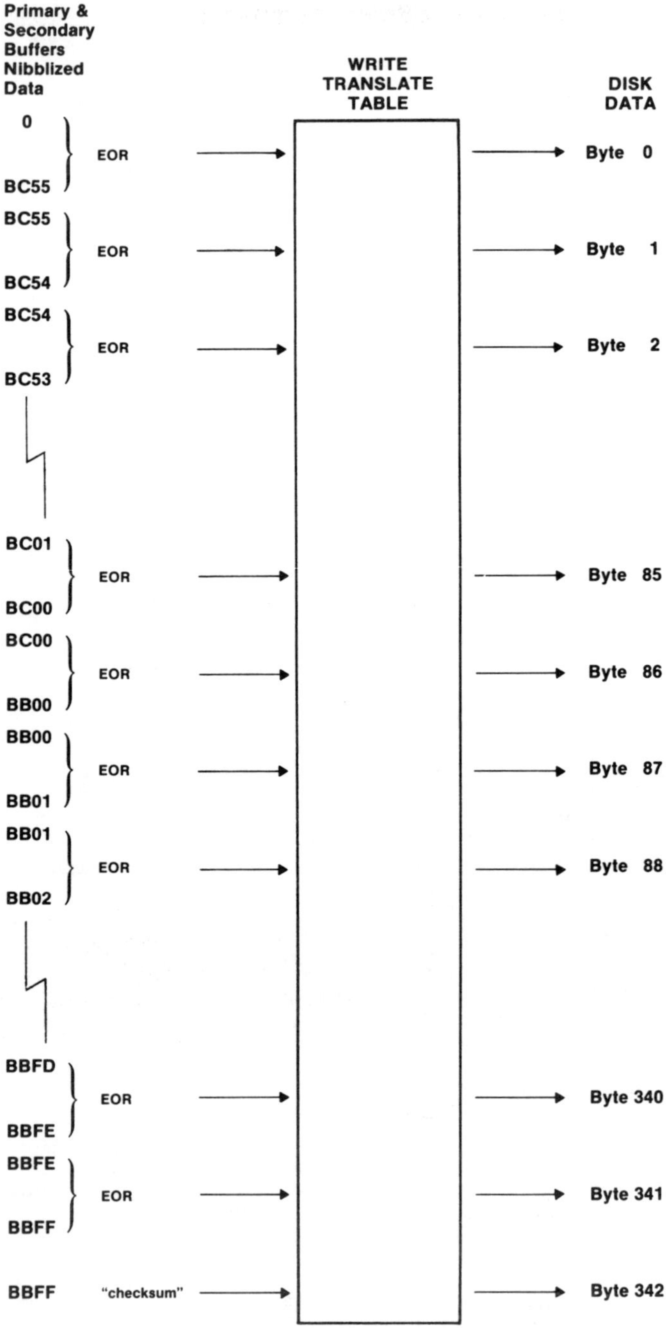

FIGURE 3.20

READING FROM DISKETTE, DOS 3.3

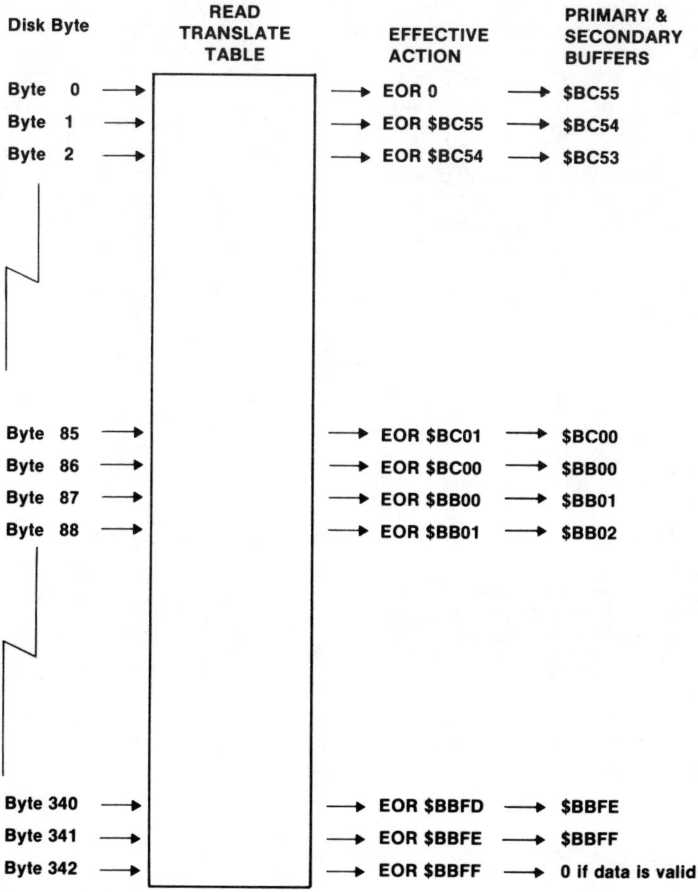

FIGURE 3.21

The third encoding technique, currently used by DOS 3.3, is similar to the "5 and 3". It was made possible by a change in the hardware which eased the requirements for valid data somewhat. The high bit must still be set, but now the byte may contain one (and only one) pair of consecutive zero bits. This allows a greater number of valid bytes and permits the use of a "6 and 2" encoding technique. A six bit byte would have the form 00XXXXXX and has values from $00 to $3F for a total of 64 different values. With the new, relaxed requirements for valid "disk" bytes there are 70 different bytes ranging in value from $95 up to $FF. After removing the two reserved bytes, $AA and $D5, there are still 68 "disk" bytes with only 64 needed. So an additional requirement was introduced to force the mapping to be one to one, namely, that there must be at least two adjacent bits set, excluding bit 7. This eliminates four more bytes and produces exactly 64 valid "disk" values. The initial transformation is done by the prenibble routine (still located at $B800) and its results are shown in Figure 3.22.

"6 and 2" PRENIBBILIZING

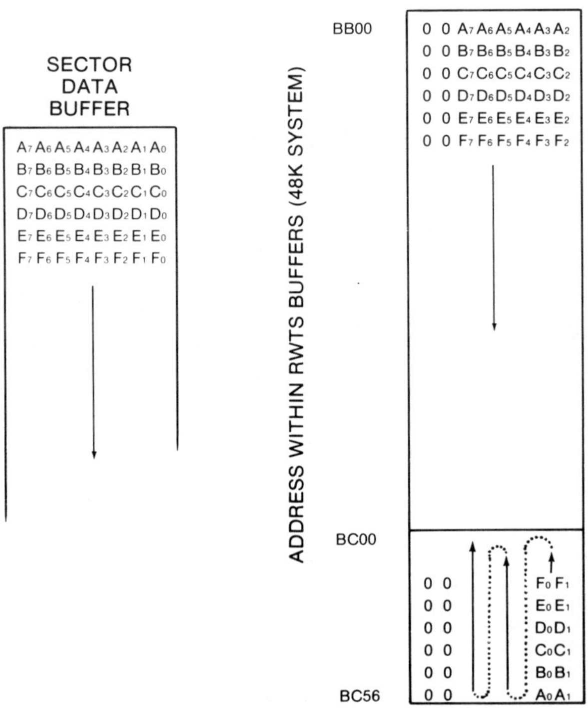

FIGURE 3.22

IT'S QUITE SIMPLE, - "6 AND 2" IS LESS THAN "5 AND 3".

A total of 342 bytes are needed, shown by finding the total number of bits (256 x 8 = 2048) and dividing by the number of bits per byte (2048 / 6 = 341.33). The transformation from the six bit bytes to valid data bytes is again performed by a one to one mapping shown in Figure 3.23. Once again, the stream of data bytes written to the diskette are a product of exclusive-ORs, exactly as with the "5 and 3" technique discussed earlier.

"6 and 2"
WRITE TRANSLATE TABLE

00 = 96	10 = B4	20 = D6	30 = ED
01 = 97	11 = B5	21 = D7	31 = EE
02 = 9A	12 = B6	22 = D9	32 = EF
03 = 9B	13 = B7	23 = DA	33 = F2
04 = 9D	14 = B9	24 = DB	34 = F3
05 = 9E	15 = BA	25 = DC	35 = F4
06 = 9F	16 = BB	26 = DD	36 = F5
07 = A6	17 = BC	27 = DE	37 = F6
08 = A7	18 = BD	28 = DF	38 = F7
09 = AB	19 = BE	29 = E5	39 = F9
0A = AC	1A = BF	2A = E6	3A = FA
0B = AD	1B = CB	2B = E7	3B = FB
0C = AE	1C = CD	2C = E9	3C = FC
0D = AF	1D = CE	2D = EA	3D = FD
0E = B2	1E = CF	2E = EB	3E = FE
0F = B3	1F = D3	2F = EC	3F = FF

AA } Reserved Bytes
D5 }

FIGURE 3.23

SECTOR INTERLEAVING

Sector interleaving, or skewing, is the staggering of sectors on a track to maximize access speed. There is usually a delay between the time DOS reads or writes a sector and the time it is ready to read or write another. This delay depends upon the application program using the disk and can vary greatly. If sectors were stored on the track in sequential order, it would usually be necessary to wait a full revolution of the diskette before the next sector could be accessed. Ordering the sectors non-sequentially (skewing them) can provide improved access speeds.

On DOS 3.2.1 and earlier versions, the 13 sectors are physically skewed on the diskette. During the boot operation, sectors are loaded from the diskette in ascending sequential order. However, files generally are loaded in descending sequential order. As a result, no single skewing scheme works well for both booting and sequentially accessing a file.

A different approach has been used in DOS 3.3 in an attempt to maximize performance. The skewing is now done in software. The 16 physical sectors are numbered in ascending order (0, 1, 2, ... , 15) and are not physically skewed at all. A look-up table is used to translate a logical or soft sector number used by RWTS into the physical sector number found on the diskette. For example, if the logical sector number were a 2, this would be translated into the physical sector number 11 ($0B). Thus, RWTS treats physical sector 11 ($0B) as sector 2 for all intents and purposes. This presents no problem if RWTS is used for disk access, but would become a consideration if access were made without RWTS. DOS 3.3 uses what we refer to as a "2 descending" skew.

In an attempt to eliminate the access differences between booting and reading files, another change was made to DOS 3.3. During the boot process, DOS is loaded backwards in descending sequential order into memory, just as files are accessed. However, due to differences in the delays for booting and reading files, no single skewing scheme is optimal. For a detailed discussion of this subject refer to HOW SECTOR SKEWING CAN AFFECT DISK PERFORMANCE in the documentation for BAG OF TRICKS*.

It is interesting to point out that Pascal, Fortran, and CP/M diskettes all use software skewing also. However, each uses a different sector order. Pascal and Fortran use a 2 ascending skew and CP/M diskettes use a 3 ascending skew. A comparison of these differences is presented in Figure 3.24.

*See the last page of this book for a description of BAG OF TRICKS.

COMPARISON OF SECTOR SKEWING

PHYSICAL SECTOR	LOGICAL SECTOR		
	DOS 3.3	PASCAL	CP/M
0	0	0	0
1	7	8	B
2	E	1	6
3	6	9	1
4	D	2	C
5	5	A	7
6	C	3	2
7	4	B	D
8	B	4	8
9	3	C	3
A	A	5	E
B	2	D	9
C	9	6	4
D	1	E	F
E	8	7	A
F	F	F	5

FIGURE 3.24

CHAPTER 4
DISKETTE ORGANIZATION

As was described in CHAPTER 3, a 16 sector diskette consists of 560 data areas of 256 bytes each, called sectors. These sectors are arranged on the diskette in 35 concentric rings or tracks of 16 sectors each. The way DOS allocates these tracks of sectors is the subject of this chapter.

A file (be it APPLESOFT, INTEGER, BINARY, or TEXT type) consists of one or more sectors containing data. Since the sector is the smallest unit of allocatable space on a diskette, a file will use up at least one sector even if it is less than 256 bytes long; the remainder of the sector is wasted. Thus, a file containing 400 characters (or bytes) of data will occupy one entire sector and 144 bytes of another with 112 bytes wasted. Knowing these facts, one would expect to be able to use up to 16 times 35 times 256 or 143,360 bytes of space on a diskette for files. Actually, the largest file that can be stored is about 126,000 bytes long. The reason for this is that some of the sectors on the diskette must be used for what is called "overhead".

```
CATALOG
DISK VOLUME 001
*I 002 HELLO
 A 002 APPLESOFT PROGRAM
 T 002 TEXT FILE
 B 002 BINARY FILE
```

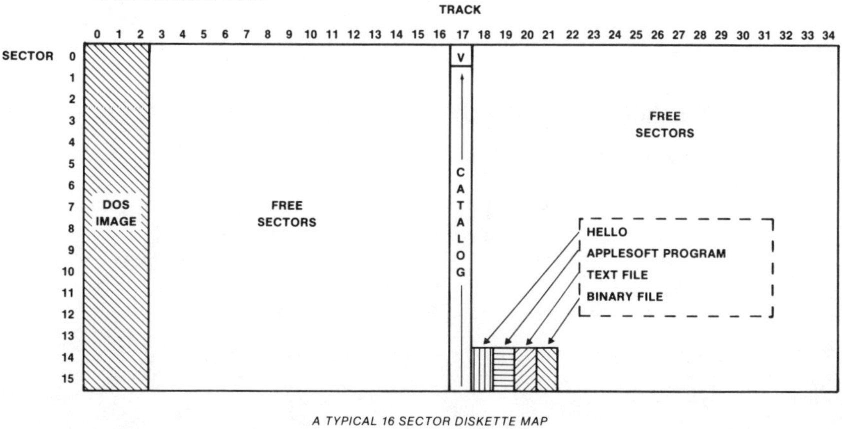

A TYPICAL 16 SECTOR DISKETTE MAP

FIGURE 4.1

Overhead sectors contain the image of DOS which is loaded when booting the diskette, a list of the names and locations of the files on the diskette, and an accounting of the sectors which are free for use with new files or expansions of existing files. An example of the way DOS uses sectors is given in Figure 4.1.

DISKETTE SPACE ALLOCATION

The map in Figure 4.1 shows that the first three tracks of each diskette are always reserved for the bootstrap image of DOS. In the exact center track (track 17) is the VTOC and catalog. The reason for placing the catalog here is simple. Since the greatest delay when using the disk is waiting for the arm to move from track to track, it is advantageous to minimize this arm movement whenever possible. By placing the catalog in the exact center track of the disk, the arm need never travel more than 17 tracks to get to the catalog track. As files are allocated on a diskette, they occupy the tracks just above the catalog track first. When the last track, track 34, has been used, track 16, the track adjacent and below the catalog, is used next, then 15, 14, 13, and so on, moving away from the catalog again, toward the DOS image tracks. If there are very few files on the diskette, they will all be clustered, hopefully, near the catalog and arm movement will be minimized. Additional space for a file, if it is needed, is first allocated in the same track occupied by the file. When that track is full, another track is allocated elsewhere on the disk in the manner described above.

THE VTOC

The Volume Table Of Contents is the "anchor" of the entire diskette. On any diskette accessible by any version of DOS, the VTOC sector is always in the same place; track 17, sector 0. (Some protected disks have the VTOC at another location and provide a special DOS which can find it.) Since files can end up anywhere on the diskette, it is through the VTOC anchor that DOS is able to find them. The VTOC of a diskette has the following format (all byte offsets are given in base 16, hexadecimal):

VOLUME TABLE OF CONTENTS (VTOC) FORMAT

BYTE	DESCRIPTION
00	Not used
01	Track number of first catalog sector
02	Sector number of first catalog sector
03	Release number of DOS used to INIT this diskette
04-05	Not used
06	Diskette volume number (1-254)
07-26	Not used
27	Maximum number of track/sector pairs which will fit in one file track/sector list sector (122 for 256 byte sectors)

28-2F	Not used
30	Last track where sectors were allocated
31	Direction of track allocation (+1 or -1)
32-33	Not used
34	Number of tracks per diskette (normally 35)
35	Number of sectors per track (13 or 16)
36-37	Number of bytes per sector (LO/HI format)
38-3B	Bit map of free sectors in track 0
3C-3F	Bit map of free sectors in track 1
40-43	Bit map of free sectors in track 2
	...
BC-BF	Bit map of free sectors in track 33
C0-C3	Bit map of free sectors in track 34
C4-FF	Bit maps for additional tracks if there are more than 35 tracks per diskette

BIT MAPS OF FREE SECTORS ON A GIVEN TRACK

A four byte binary string of ones and zeros, representing free and allocated sectors respectively. Hexadecimal sector numbers are assigned to bit positions as follows:

BYTE	SECTORS
+0	FEDC BA98
+1	7654 3210
+2	.... (not used)
+3	.... (not used)

Thus, if only sectors E and 8 are free and all others are allocated, the bit map will be:

41000000

If all sectors are free:

FFFF0000

An example of a VTOC sector is given in Figure 4.2. This VTOC corresponds to the map of the diskette given in Figure 4.1.

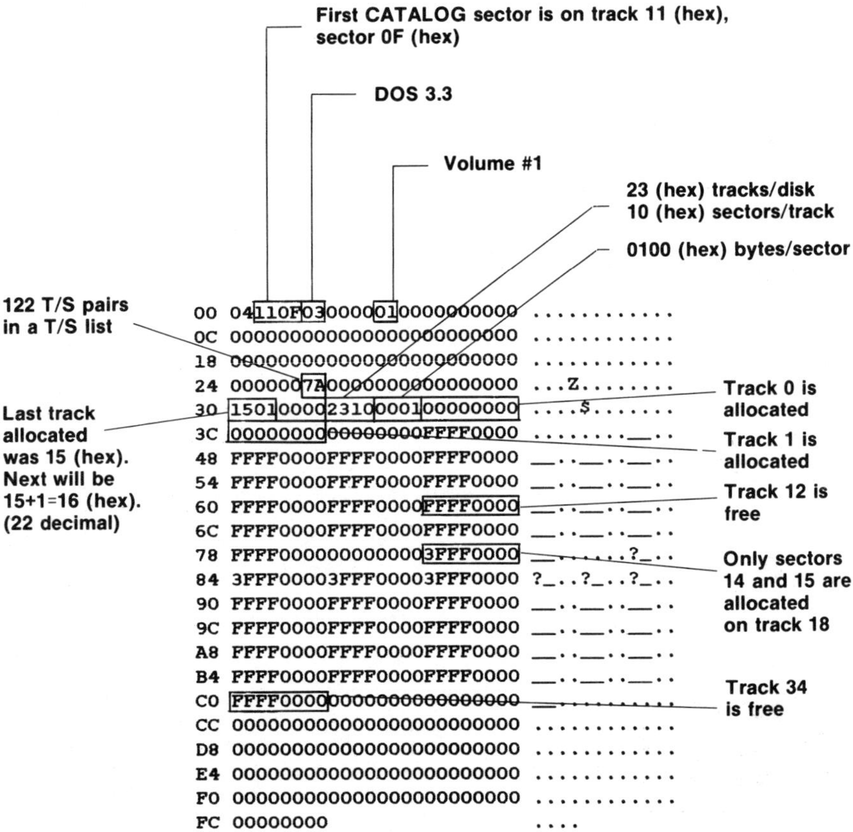

FIGURE 4.2 — EXAMPLE VTOC

THE CATALOG

In order for DOS to find a given file, it must first read the VTOC to find out where the first catalog sector is located. Typically, the catalog sectors for a diskette are the remaining sectors on track 17, following the VTOC sector. Of course, as long as a track/sector pointer exists in the VTOC and the VTOC is located at track 17, sector 0, DOS does not really care where the catalog resides. Figure 4.3 diagrams the catalog track. The figure shows the track/sector pointer in the VTOC at bytes 01 and 02 as an arrow pointing to track 17 (11 in hexadecimal) sector F. The last sector in the track is the first catalog sector and describes the first seven files on the diskette. Each catalog sector has a track/sector pointer in the same position (bytes 01 and 02) which points to the next catalog sector. The last catalog sector (sector 1) has a zero pointer to indicate that there are no more catalog sectors in the chain.

In each catalog sector up to seven files may be listed and described. Thus, on a typical DOS 3.3 diskette, the catalog can hold up to 15 times 7, or 105 files. A catalog sector is formatted as described on the following page.

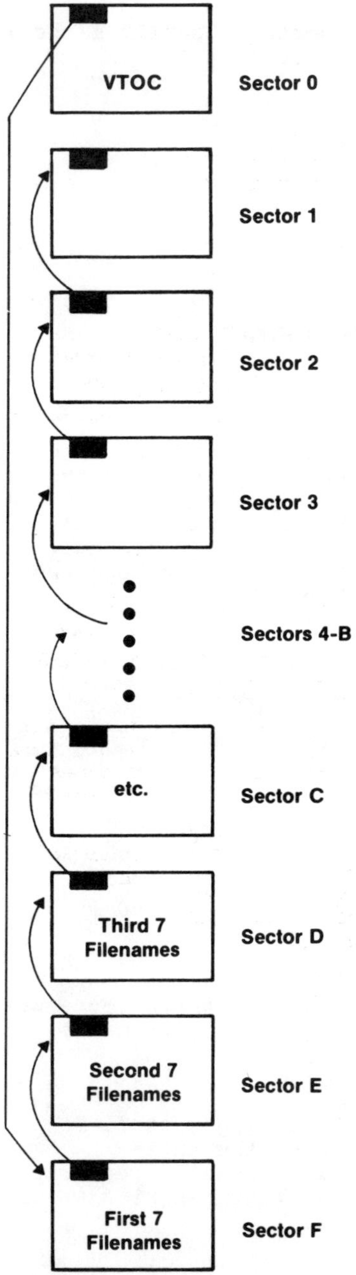

FIGURE 4.3 — TRACK 17, THE CATALOG TRACK

CATALOG SECTOR FORMAT

BYTE	DESCRIPTION
00	Not used
01	Track number of next catalog sector (usually 11 hex)
02	Sector number of next catalog sector
03-0A	Not used
0B-2D	First file descriptive entry
2E-50	Second file descriptive entry
51-73	Third file descriptive entry
74-96	Fourth file descriptive entry
97-B9	Fifth file descriptive entry
BA-DC	Sixth file descriptive entry
DD-FF	Seventh file descriptive entry

FILE DESCRIPTIVE ENTRY FORMAT

RELATIVE BYTE	DESCRIPTION
00	Track of first track/sector list sector. If this is a deleted file, this byte contains a hex FF and the original track number is copied to the last byte of the file name field (BYTE 20). If this byte contains a hex 00, the entry is assumed to never have been used and is available for use. (This means track 0 can never be used for data even if the DOS image is "wiped" from the diskette.)
01	Sector of first track/sector list sector
02	File type and flags: Hex 80+file type - file is locked 00+file type - file is not locked 00 - TEXT file 01 - INTEGER BASIC file 02 - APPLESOFT BASIC file 04 - BINARY file 08 - S type file 10 - RELOCATABLE object module file 20 - A type file 40 - B type file (thus, 84 is a locked BINARY file, and 90 is a locked R type file)
03-20	File name (30 characters)
21-22	Length of file in sectors (LO/HI format). The CATALOG command will only format the LO byte of this length giving 1-255 but a full 65,535 may be stored here.

Figure 4.4 is an example of a typical catalog sector. In this example there are only four files on the entire diskette, so only one catalog sector was needed to describe them. There are four entries in use and three entries which have never been used and contain zeros.

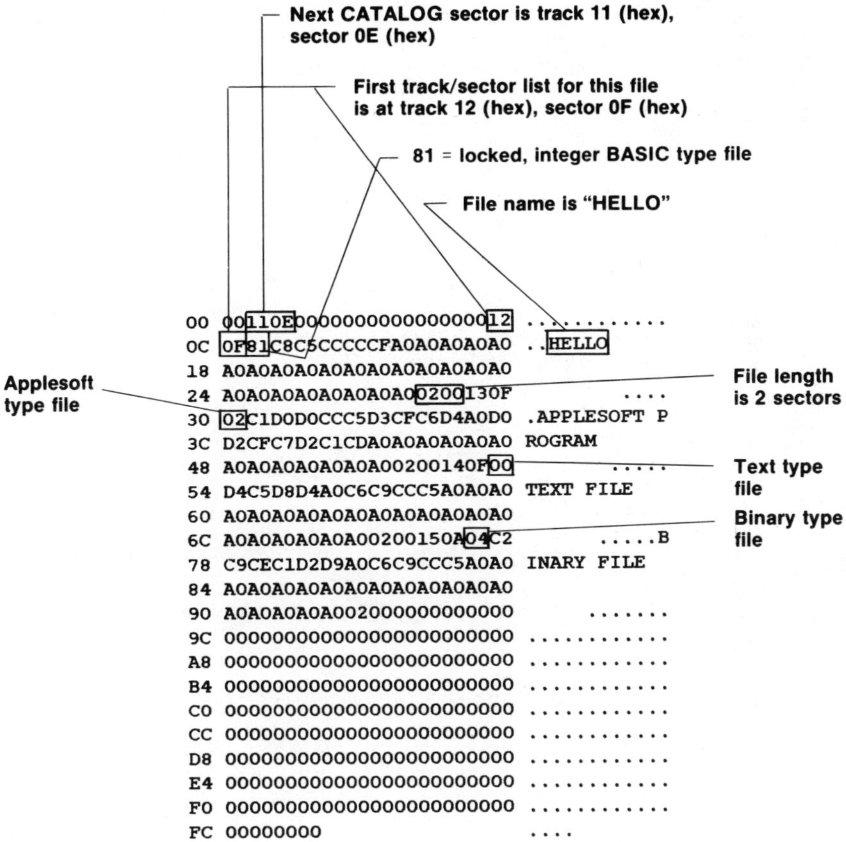

FIGURE 4.4 — EXAMPLE CATALOG SECTOR

THE TRACK/SECTOR LIST

Each file has associated with it a "Track/Sector List" sector. This sector contains a list of track/sector pointer pairs which sequentially list the data sectors which make up the file. The file descriptive entry in the catalog sector points to this T/S List sector which, in turn, points to each sector in the file. This concept is diagramed in Figure 4.5.

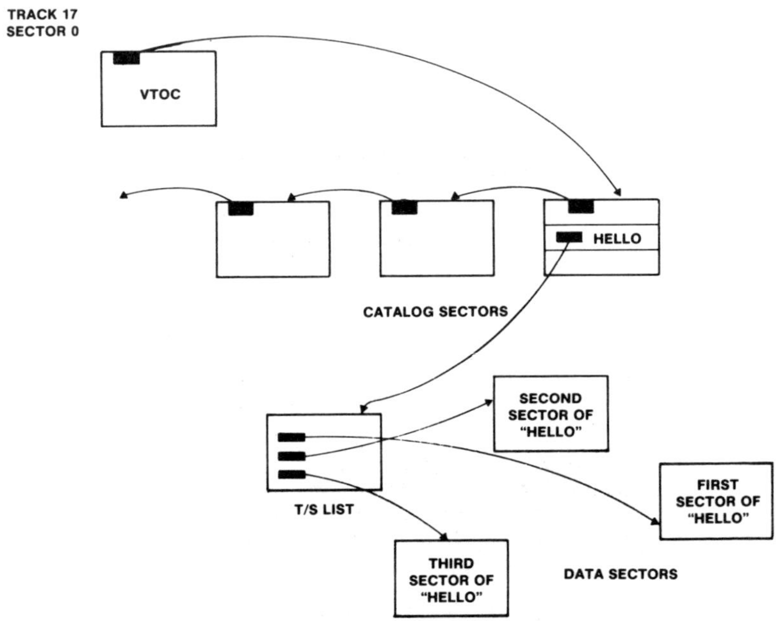

FIGURE 4.5 - PATH DOS MUST FOLLOW TO FIND A FILE

The format of a Track/Sector List sector is given below. Note that since even a minimal file requires one T/S List sector and one data sector, the least number of sectors a non-empty file can have is 2. Also, note that a very large file, having more than 122 data sectors, will need more than one Track/Sector List to hold all the Track/Sector pointer pairs.

TRACK/SECTOR LIST FORMAT

BYTE	DESCRIPTION
00	Not used
01	Track number of next T/S List sector if one was needed or zero if no more T/S List sectors.
02	Sector number of next T/S List sector (if present).
03-04	Not used

05-06	Sector offset in file of the first sector described by this list.
07-0B	Not used
0C-0D	Track and sector of first data sector or zeros
0E-0F	Track and sector of second data sector or zeros
10-FF	Up to 120 more Track/Sector pairs

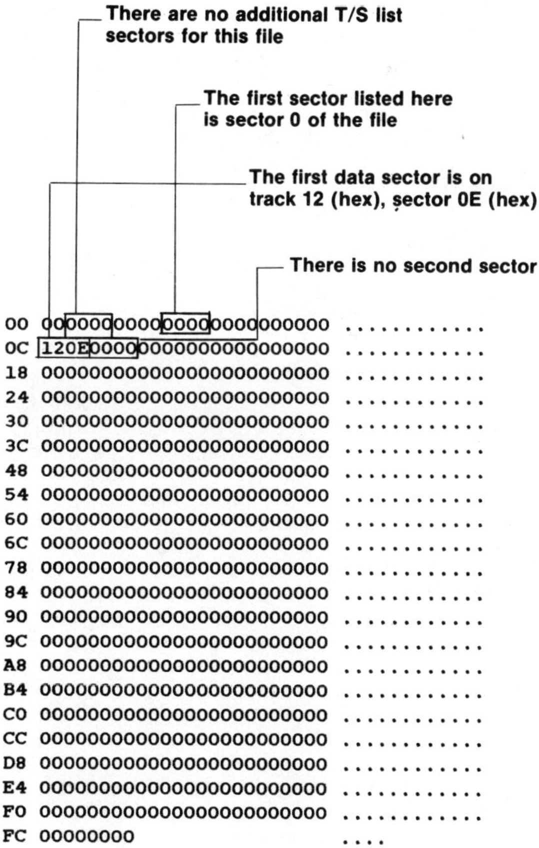

FIGURE 4.6 — EXAMPLE TRACK/SECTOR LIST

A sequential file will end when the first zero T/S List entry is encountered. A random file, however, can have spaces within it which were never allocated and therefore have no data sectors allocated in the T/S List. This distinction is not always handled correctly by DOS. The VERIFY command, for instance, stops when it gets to the first zero T/S List entry and can not be used to verify some random organization text files.

An example T/S List sector is given in Figure 4.6. The example file (HELLO, from our previous examples) has only one data sector, since it is less than 256 bytes in length. Counting this data sector and the T/S List sector, HELLO is 2 sectors long, and this will be the value shown when a CATALOG command is done.

Following the Track/Sector pointer in the T/S List sector, we come to the first data sector of the file. As we examine the data sectors, the differences between the file types become apparent. All files (except, perhaps, a random TEXT file) are considered to be continuous streams of data, even though they must be broken up into 256 byte chunks to fit in sectors on the diskette. Although these sectors are not necessarily contiguous (or next to each other on the diskette), by using the Track/Sector List, DOS can read each sector of the file in the correct order so that the programmer need never know that the data was broken up into sectors at all.

TEXT FILES

The TEXT data type is the least complicated file data structure. It consists of one or more records, separated from each other by carriage return characters (hex 8D's). This structure is diagrammed and an example file is given in Figure 4.7. Usually, the end of a TEXT file is signaled by the presence of a hex 00 or the lack of any more data sectors in the T/S List for the file. As mentioned earlier, if the file has random organization, there may be hex 00's imbedded in the data and even missing data sectors in areas where nothing was ever written. In this case, the only way to find the end of the file is to scan the Track/Sector List for the last non-zero Track/Sector pair. Since carriage return characters and hex 00's have special meaning in a TEXT type file, they can not be part of the data itself. For this reason, and to make the data accessible to BASIC, the data can only contain printable or ASCII characters (alphabetics, numerics or special characters, see p. 8 in the APPLE II REFERENCE MANUAL) This restriction makes processing of a TEXT file slower and less efficient in the use of disk space than with a BINARY type file, since each digit must occupy a full byte in the file.

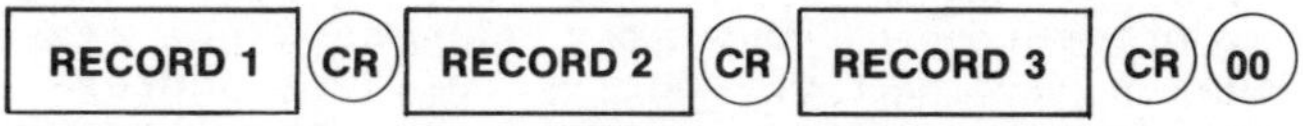

A Sequential Text Type File

Record 1   CR   End of file

```
00 B1ACB2ACB3ACB48D00000000 1,2,3,4.....
0C 000000000000000000000000 ............
18 000000000000000000000000 ............
24 000000000000000000000000 ............
30 000000000000000000000000 ............
3C 000000000000000000000000 ............
48 000000000000000000000000 ............
54 000000000000000000000000 ............
60 000000000000000000000000 ............
6C 000000000000000000000000 ............
78 000000000000000000000000 ............
84 000000000000000000000000 ............
90 000000000000000000000000 ............
9C 000000000000000000000000 ............
A8 000000000000000000000000 ............
B4 000000000000000000000000 ............
C0 000000000000000000000000 ............
CC 000000000000000000000000 ............
D8 000000000000000000000000 ............
E4 000000000000000000000000 ............
F0 000000000000000000000000 ............
FC 00000000                 ....
```

Example Text File Sector

FIGURE 4.7 — TEXT FILE DATA TYPE

BINARY FILES

The structure of a BINARY type file is shown in Figure 4.8. An exact copy of the memory involved is written to the disk sector(s), preceded by the memory address where it was found and the length (a total of four bytes). The address and length (in low order, high order format) are those given in the A and L keywords from the BSAVE command which created the file. Notice that DOS writes one extra byte to the file. This does not matter too much since BLOAD and BRUN will only read the number of bytes given in the length field. (Of course, if you BSAVE a multiple of 256 bytes, a sector will be wasted because of this error) DOS could be made to BLOAD or BRUN the binary image at a different address either by providing the A (address) keyword when the command is entered, or by changing the address in the first two bytes of the file on the diskette.

APPLESOFT AND INTEGER FILES

A BASIC program, be it APPLESOFT or INTEGER, is saved to the diskette in a way that is similar to BSAVE. The format of an APPLESOFT file type is given in Figure 4.9 and that of INTEGER BASIC in 4.10. When the SAVE command is typed, DOS determines the location of the BASIC program image in memory and its length. Since a BASIC program is always loaded at a location known to the BASIC interpreter, it is not necessary to store the address in the file as with a BINARY file. The length is stored, however, as the first two bytes, and is followed by the image from memory. Notice that, again, DOS incorrectly writes an additional byte, even though it will be ignored by LOAD. The memory image of the program consists of program lines in an internal format which is made up of what are called "tokens". A treatment of the structure of a BASIC program as it appears in memory is outside the scope of this manual, but a breakdown of the example INTEGER BASIC program is given in Figure 4.10.

OTHER FILE TYPES (S,R, new A, new B)

Additional file types have been defined within DOS as can be seen in the file descriptive entry format, shown earlier. No DOS commands at present use these additional types so their eventual meaning is anybody's guess. The R file type, however, has been used with the DOS TOOLKIT assembler for its output file, a relocatable object module. This file type is used with a special form of BINARY file which can contain the memory image of a machine language program which may be relocated anywhere in the machine based on additional information stored with the image itself. The format for this type of file is given in the documentation accompanying the DOS TOOLKIT. It is recommended that if the reader requires more information about R files he should refer to that documentation.

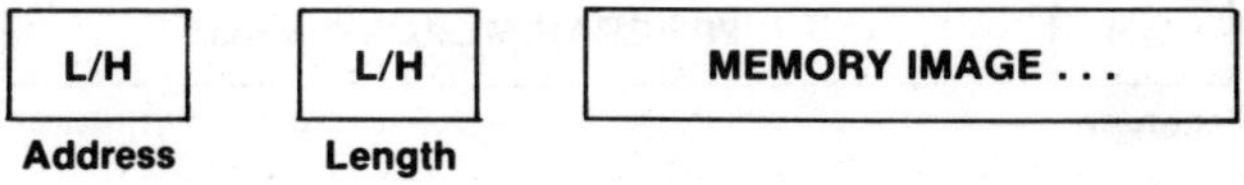

A Binary Type File

Start address = 03D0 (hex)

File length = 0030 (hex)

Binary memory image

```
00 D0033000 4CBF9D4C849D4CFD P.O.L?.L..L]
0C AA4CB5B7AD0F9DAC0E9D60AD *L57-..,..`-
18 C2AAACC1AA604C51A8EAEA4C B*,A*`LQ(JJL
24 59FABF9D384C58FF4C65FF4C YZ?.8LX_Le_L
30 65FF65FFBE00000000000000 e_e_>.......
3C 000000000000000000000000 ............
48 000000000000000000000000 ............
54 000000000000000000000000 ............
60 000000000000000000000000 ............
6C 000000000000000000000000 ............
78 000000000000000000000000 ............
84 000000000000000000000000 ............
90 000000000000000000000000 ............
9C 000000000000000000000000 ............
A8 000000000000000000000000 ............
B4 000000000000000000000000 ............
C0 000000000000000000000000 ............
CC 000000000000000000000000 ............
D8 000000000000000000000000 ............
E4 000000000000000000000000 ............
F0 000000000000000000000000 ............
FC 00000000                 ....
```

Example Binary File Sector

FIGURE 4.8 — BINARY FILE DATA TYPE

L/H	PROGRAM MEMORY IMAGE
Length	

An Applesoft Type File

```
10 PRINT   "[CTRL-D] OPEN TEXT FILE"
20 PRINT   "[CTRL-D] WRITE TEXT FILE"
30 PRINT   "1,2,3,4"
40 PRINT   "[CTRL-D] CLOSE TEXT FILE"
50  END
```

Program is 5E (hex) bytes long

Applesoft program

```
00 5E0018080A00BA22044F5045 ^.....:".OPE
0C 4E2054455854204649 4C4522 N TEXT FILE"
18 0030081400BA220457524954 .0...:".WRIT
24 452054455854204649 4C4522 E TEXT FILE"
30 003F081E00BA22312C322C33 .?...:"1,2,3
3C 2C34220057082800BA220443 ,4".W.(.:".C
48 4C4F53452054455854204649 LOSE TEXT FI
54 4C4522005D08320080000000 LE".].2.....
60 640000000000000000000000 d...........
6C 000000000000000000000000 ............
78 000000000000000000000000 ............
84 000000000000000000000000 ............
90 000000000000000000000000 ............
9C 000000000000000000000000 ............
A8 000000000000000000000000 ............
B4 000000000000000000000000 ............
C0 000000000000000000000000 ............
CC 000000000000000000000000 ............
D8 000000000000000000000000 ............
E4 000000000000000000000000 ............
F0 000000000000000000000000 ............
FC 00000000                 ....
```

Example Applesoft File Sector

FIGURE 4.9 — APPLESOFT BASIC FILE TYPE

L/H	PROGRAM MEMORY IMAGE
Length	

An Integer Type File

10 END

Program is 5 bytes long

Length of line (5 bytes)

Line number (hex 0A = 10 decimal)

"Tokens" { **51 = END**, **01 = end of line** }

```
00 0500050A0051010500000000 .....Q......
0C 000000000000000000000000 ............
18 000000000000000000000000 ............
30 000000000000000000000000 ............
3C 000000000000000000000000 ............
48 000000000000000000000000 ............
54 000000000000000000000000 ............
60 000000000000000000000000 ............
6C 000000000000000000000000 ............
78 000000000000000000000000 ............
84 000000000000000000000000 ............
90 000000000000000000000000 ............
9C 000000000000000000000000 ............
A8 000000000000000000000000 ............
B4 000000000000000000000000 ............
C0 000000000000000000000000 ............
CC 000000000000000000000000 ............
D8 000000000000000000000000 ............
E4 000000000000000000000000 ............
F0 000000000000000000000000 ............
FC 00000000                 ....
```

Example Integer File Sector

FIGURE 4.10 — INTEGER BASIC FILE TYPE

EMERGENCY REPAIRS

From time to time the information on a diskette can become damaged or lost. This can create various symptoms, ranging from mild side effects, such as the disk not booting, to major problems, such as an input/output (I/O) error in the catalog. A good understanding of the format of a diskette, as described previously, and a few program tools can allow any reasonably sharp APPLE II user to patch up most errors on his diskettes.

A first question would be, "how do errors occur". The most common cause of an error is a worn or physically damaged diskette. Usually, a diskette will warn you that it is wearing out by producing "soft errors". Soft errors are I/O errors which occur only randomly. You may get an I/O error message when you catalog a disk one time and have it catalog correctly if you try again. When this happens, the smart programmer immediately copies the files on the aged diskette to a brand new one and discards the old one or keeps it as a backup.

EMERGENCY REPAIRS ARE EASIER IF YOU HAVE A BACKUP.

Another cause of damaged diskettes is the practice of hitting the RESET key to abort the execution of a program which is accessing the diskette. Damage will usually occur when the RESET signal comes just as data is being written onto the disk. Powering the machine off just as data is being written to the disk is also a sure way to clobber a diskette. Of course, real hardware problems in the disk drive or controller card and ribbon cable can cause damage as well.

If the damaged diskette can be cataloged, recovery is much easier. A damaged DOS image in the first three tracks can usually be corrected by running the MASTER CREATE program against the diskette or by copying all the files to another diskette. If only one file produces an I/O error when it is VERIFYed, it may be possible to copy most of the sectors of the file to another diskette by skipping over the bad sector with an assembler program which calls RWTS in DOS or with a BASIC program (if the file is a TEXT file). Indeed, if the problem is a bad checksum (see CHAPTER 3) it may be possible to read the bad sector and ignore the error and get most of the data.

An I/O error usually means that one of two conditions has occurred. Either a bad checksum was detected on the data in a sector, meaning that one or more bytes is bad; or the sectoring is clobbered such that the sector no longer even exists on the diskette. If the latter is the case, the diskette (or at the very least, the track) must be reformatted, resulting in a massive loss of data. Although DOS can be patched to format a single track, it is usually easier to copy all readable sectors from the damaged diskette to another formatted diskette and then reconstruct the lost data there.

Disk utilities, such as Quality Software's BAG OF TRICKS, allow the user to read and display the contents of sectors. BAG OF TRICKS will also allow you to modify the sector data and rewrite it to the same or another diskette. If you do not have BAG OF TRICKS or another commercial disk utility, you can use the ZAP program in APPENDIX A of this book. The ZAP program will read any track/sector on an unprotected diskette into memory, allowing the user to examine it or modify the data and then, optionally, rewrite it to a diskette. Using such a program is very important when learning about diskette formats and when fixing clobbered data.

Using ZAP, a bad sector within a file can be localized by reading each track/sector listed in the T/S List sector for the file. If the bad sector is a catalog sector, the pointers of up to seven files may be lost. When this occurs, a search of the diskette can be made to find T/S List sectors which do not correspond to any files listed in the remaining "good" catalog sectors. As these sectors are found, new file descriptive entries can be made in the damaged sector which point to these T/S Lists. When the entire catalog is lost, this process can take hours, even with a good understanding of the format of DOS diskettes. Such an endeavor should only be undertaken if there is no other way to recover the data. Of course the best policy is to create backup copies of important files periodically to simplify recovery. More information on the above procedures is given in APPENDIX A.

A less significant form of diskette clobber, but very annoying, is the loss of free sectors. Since DOS allocates an entire track of sectors at a time while a file is open, hitting RESET can cause these sectors to be marked in use in the VTOC even though they have not yet been added to any T/S List. These lost sectors can never be recovered by normal means, even when the file is deleted, since they are not in its T/S List. The result is a DISK FULL message before the diskette is actually full. To reclaim the lost sectors it is necessary to compare every sector listed in every T/S List against the VTOC bit map to see if there are any discrepancies. There are utility programs which will do this automatically but the best way to solve this problem is to copy all the files on the diskette to another diskette (note that FID must be used, not COPY, since COPY copies an image of the diskette, bad VTOC and all).

If a file is deleted it can usually be recovered, providing that additional sector allocations have not occured since it was deleted. If another file was created after the DELETE command, DOS might have reused some or all of the sectors of the old file. The catalog can be quickly ZAPped to move the track number of the T/S List from byte 20 of the file descriptive entry to byte 0. The file should then be copied to another disk and then the original deleted so that the VTOC freespace bit map will be updated.

CHAPTER 5
THE STRUCTURE OF DOS

DOS MEMORY USE

DOS is an assembly language program which is loaded into RAM memory when the user boots his disk. If the diskette booted is a master diskette, the DOS image is loaded into the last possible part of RAM memory, dependent upon the size of the actual machine on which it is run. By doing this, DOS fools the active BASIC into believing that there is actually less RAM memory on the machine than there is. On a 48K APPLE II with DOS active, for instance, BASIC believes that there is only about 38K of RAM. DOS does this by adjusting HIMEM after it is loaded to prevent BASIC from using the memory DOS is occupying. If a slave diskette is booted, DOS is loaded into whatever RAM it occupied when the slave diskette was INITialized. If the slave was created on a 16K APPLE, DOS will be loaded in the 6 to 16K range of RAM, even if the machine now has 48K. In this case, the APPLE will appear, for all intents an purposes, to have only 6K of RAM. If the slave was created on a 48K system, it will not boot on less than 48K since the RAM DOS occupied does not exist on a smaller machine.

A diagram of DOS's memory for a 48K APPLE II is given in Figure 5.1. As can be seen, there are four major divisions to the memory occupied by DOS. The first 1.75K is used for file buffers. With the default of MAXFILES 3, there are three file buffers set aside here. Each buffer occupies 595 bytes and corresponds to one potentially open file. File buffers are also used by DOS to LOAD and SAVE files, etc. If MAXFILES is changed from 3, the space occupied by the file buffers also changes. This affects the placement of HIMEM, moving it up or down with fewer or more buffers respectively.

The 3.5K above the file buffers is occupied by the main DOS routines. It is here that DOS's executable machine language code begins. The main routines are responsible for initializing DOS, interfacing to BASIC, interpreting commands, and managing the file buffers. All disk functions are passed on via subroutine calls to the file manager.

The file manager, occupying about 2.8K, is a collection of subroutines which perform almost any function needed to access a disk file. Functions include: OPEN, CLOSE, READ, WRITE, POSITION, DELETE, CATALOG, LOCK, UNLOCK, RENAME, INIT, and VERIFY. Although the file manager is a subroutine of DOS it may also be called by a user written assembly lanaguage program which is not part of DOS. This interface is generalized through a group of vectors in page 3 of RAM and is documented in the next chapter.

The last 2.5K of DOS is the Read/Write Track/Sector (RWTS) package. RWTS is the next step lower in protocol from the file manager - in fact it is called as a subroutine by the file manager. Where the file manager deals with files, RWTS deals with tracks and sectors on the diskette. A typical call to RWTS would be to read track 17 sector 0 or to write 256 bytes of data in memory onto track 5 sector E. An external interface is also provided for access to RWTS from a user written assembly language program and is described in the next chapter.

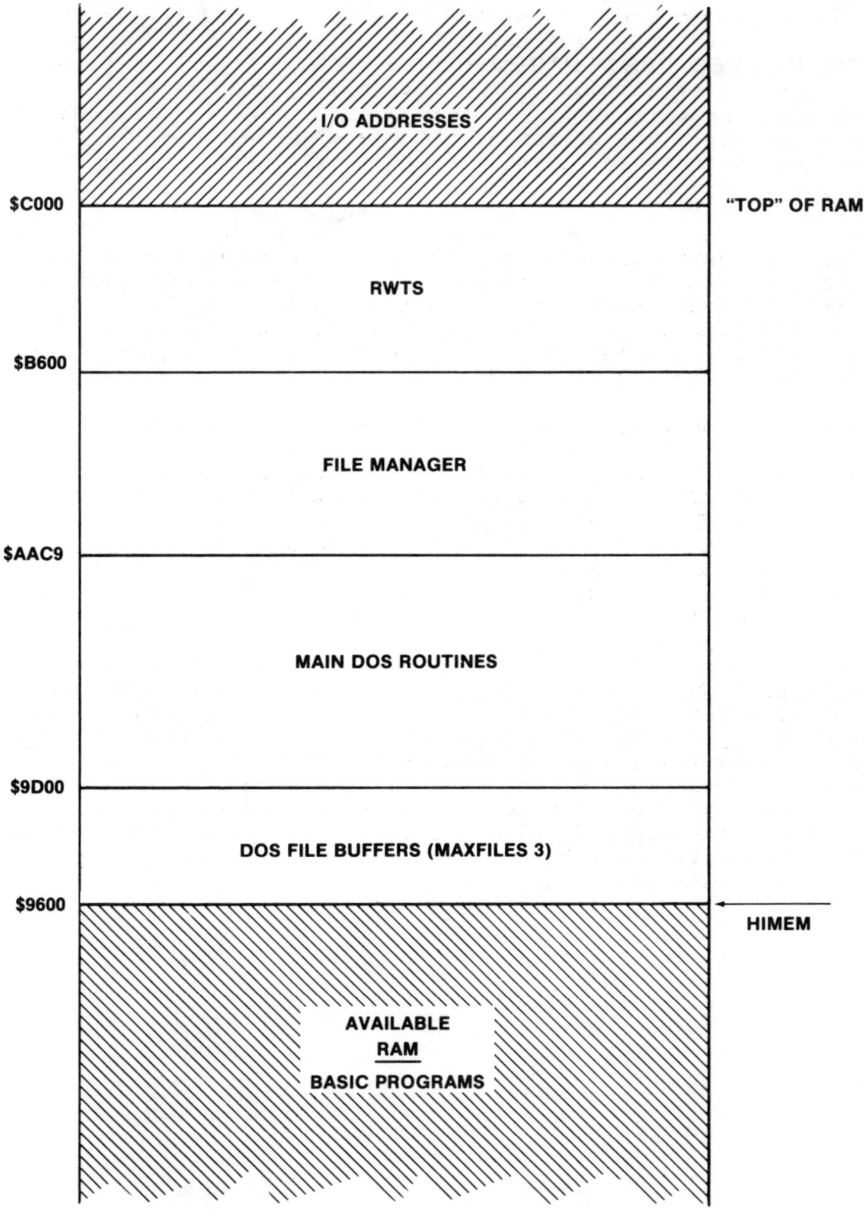

FIGURE 5.1 — DOS MEMORY USE (48K APPLE)

THE DOS VECTORS IN PAGE 3

In addition to the approximately 10K of RAM occupied by DOS in high memory, DOS maintains a group of what are called "vectors" in page 3 of low memory ($300 through $3FF). These vectors allow access to certain places within the DOS collection of routines via a fixed location ($3D0 for instance). Because DOS may be loaded in various locations, depending upon the size of the machine and whether a slave or master diskette is booted, the addresses of the externally callable subroutines within DOS will change. By putting the addresses of these routines in a vector at a fixed location, dependencies on DOS's location in memory are eliminated. The page 3 vector table is also useful in locating subroutines within DOS which may not be in the same memory location for different versions of DOS. Locations $300 through $3CF were used by earlier versions of DOS during the boot process to load the Boot 1 program but are used by DOS 3.3 as a data buffer and disk code translate table. Presumably, this change was made to provide more memory for the first bootstrap loader (more on this later). The vector table itself starts at $3D0.

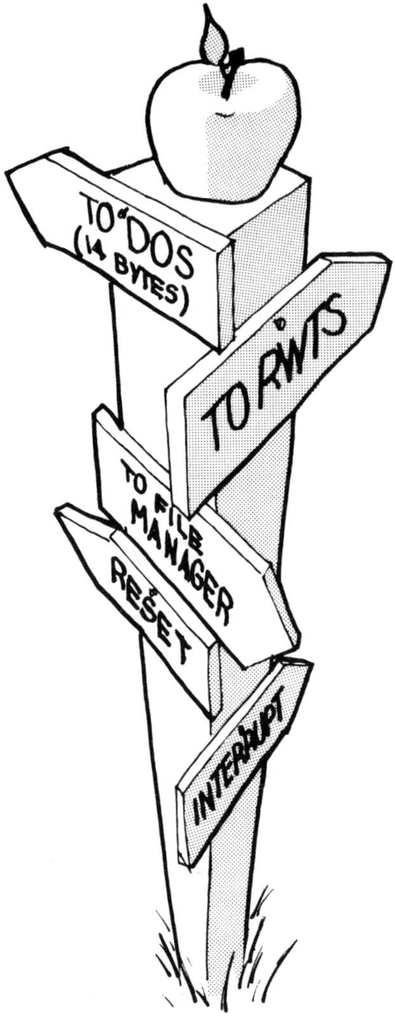

DOS VECTORS

DOS VECTOR TABLE ($3D0-$3FF)

ADDR	USAGE
3D0	A JMP (jump or GOTO) instruction to the DOS warmstart routine. This routine reenters DOS but does not discard the current BASIC program and does not reset MAXFILES or other DOS environmental variables.
3D3	A JMP to the DOS coldstart routine. This routine reinitializes DOS as if it was rebooted, clearing the current BASIC file and resetting HIMEM.
3D6	A JMP to the DOS file manager subroutine to allow a user written assembly language program to call it.
3D9	A JMP to the DOS Read/Write Track/Sector (RWTS) routine to allow user written assembly language programs to call it.
3DC	A short subroutine which locates the input parameter list for the file manager to allow a user written program to set up input parameters before calling the file manager.
3E3	A short subroutine which locates the input parameter list for RWTS to allow a user written program to set up input parameters before calling RWTS.
3EA	A JMP to the DOS subroutine which "reconnects" the DOS intercepts to the keyboard and screen data streams.
3EF	A JMP to the routine which will handle a BRK machine language instruction. This vector is only supported by the AUTOSTART ROM. Normally the vector contains the address of the monitor ROM subroutine which displays the registers.
3F2	LO/HI address of routine which will handle RESET for the AUTOSTART ROM. Normally the DOS restart address is stored here but the user may change it if he wishes to handle RESET himself.
3F4	Power-up byte. Contains a "funny complement" of the RESET address with a $A5. This scheme is used to determine if the machine was just powered up or if RESET was pressed. If a power-up occured, the AUTOSTART ROM ignores the address at 3F2 (since it has never been initialized) and attempts to boot a diskette. To prevent this from happening when you change $3F2 to handle your own RESETs, EOR (exclusive OR) the new value at $3F3 with a $A5 and store the result in the power-up byte.
3F5	A JMP to a machine language routine which is to be called when the '&' feature is used in APPLESOFT.
3F8	A JMP to a machine language routine which is to be called when a control-Y is entered from the monitor.
3FB	A JMP to a machine language routine which is to be called when a non-maskable interrupt occurs.
3FE	LO/HI address of a routine which is to be called when a maskable interrupt occurs.

WHAT HAPPENS DURING BOOTING

When an APPLE is powered on its memory is essentially devoid of any programs. In order to get DOS running, a diskette is "booted". The term "boot" refers to the process of bootstrap loading DOS into RAM. Bootstrap loading involves a series of steps which load successively bigger pieces of a program until all of the program is in memory and is running. In the case of DOS, bootstrapping occurs in four stages. The location of these stages on the diskette and a memory map are given in Figure 5.2 and a description of the bootstrap process follows.

The first boot stage (let's call it Boot 0) is the execution of the ROM on the disk controller card. When the user types PR#6 or C600G or 6(ctrl)P, for instance, control is

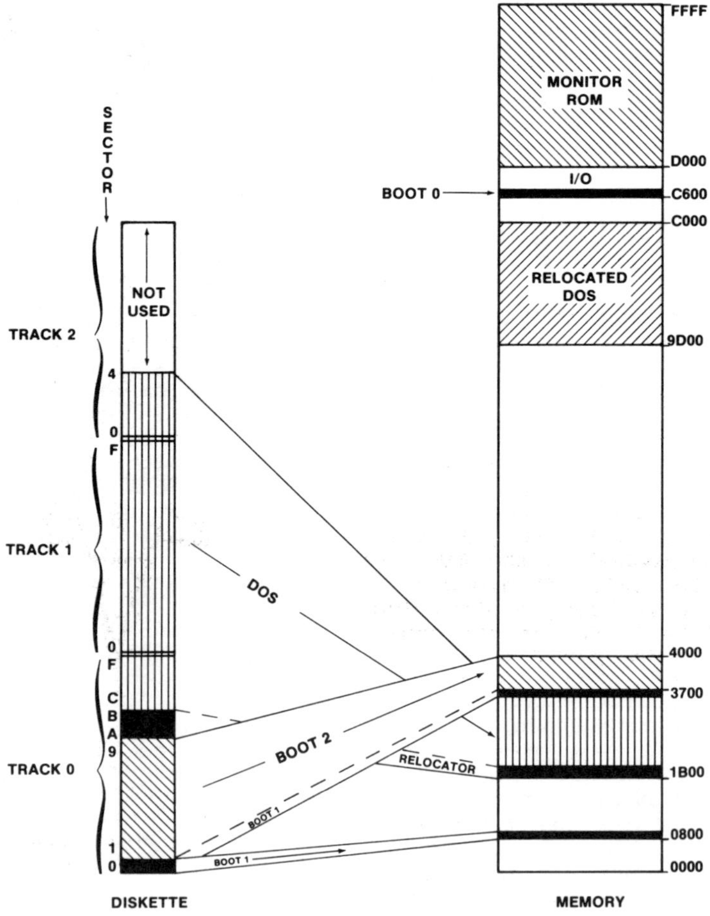

FIGURE 5.2 - BOOTSTRAP PROCESS

transfered to the disk controller ROM on the card in slot 6. This ROM is a machine language program of about 256 bytes in length. When executed, it "recalibrates" the disk arm by pulling it back to track 0 (the "clacketty-clack" noise that is heard) and then reads sector 0 from track 0 into RAM memory at location $800 (DOS 3.3. Earlier versions used $300). Once this sector is read, the first stage boot jumps (GOTO's) $800 which is the second stage boot (Boot 1).

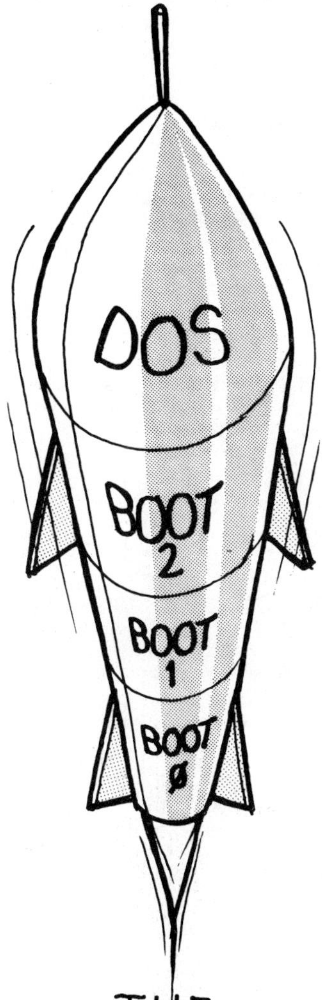

THE BOOT PROCESS

Boot 1, also about 256 bytes long, uses part of the Boot 0 ROM as a subroutine and, in a loop, reads the next nine sectors on track 0 (sectors 1 through 9) into RAM. Taken together, these sectors contain the next stage of the bootstrap process, Boot 2. Boot 2 is loaded in one of two positions in memory, depending upon whether a slave or a master diskette is being booted. If the diskette is a slave diskette, Boot 2 will be loaded 9 pages (256 bytes per page) below the end of the DOS under which the slave was INITed. Thus, if the slave was created on a 32K DOS, Boot 2 will be loaded in the RAM from $7700 to $8000. If a master diskette is being booted, Boot 2 will be loaded in the same place as for a 16K slave ($3700 to $4000). In the process of loading Boot 2, Boot 1 is loaded a second time in the page in memory right below Boot 2 ($3600 for a master diskette). This is so that, should a new diskette be INITed, a copy of Boot 1 will be available in memory to be written to its track 0 sector 0. When Boot 1 is finished loading Boot 2, it jumps there to begin execution of the next stage of the bootstrap.

Boot 2 consists of two parts: a loader "main program"; and the RWTS subroutine package. Up to this point there has been no need to move the disk arm since all of the necessary sectors have been on track 0. Now, however, more sectors must be loaded, requiring arm movement to access additional tracks. Since this complicates the disk access, RWTS is called by the Boot 2 loader to move the arm and read the sectors it needs to load the last part of the bootstrap, DOS itself. Boot 2 now locates track 2 sector 4 and reads its contents into RAM just below the image of Boot 1 (this would be at $3500 for a master diskette). In a loop, Boot 2 reads 26 more sectors into memory, each one 256 bytes before the last. The last sector (track 0 sector A) is read into $1B00 for a master diskette. The 27 sectors which were read are the image of the DOS main routines and the file manager. With the loading of these routines, all of DOS has been loaded into memory. At this point, the bootstrap process for a slave diskette is complete and a jump is taken to the DOS coldstart address. If the diskette is a master, the image of DOS is only valid if the machine is a 16K APPLE II. If more memory is present, the DOS image must be relocated into the highest possible RAM present in the machine. To do this, the master version of Boot 2 jumps to a special relocation program at $1B03. This relocator is 512 bytes in length and was automatically loaded as the two lowest pages of the DOS image. (In the case of a slave diskette, these pages contain binary zeros.) The relocator determines the size of the machine by systematically storing and loading on high RAM memory pages until it finds the last valid page. It then moves the DOS image from $1D00 to its final location ($9D00 for 48K) and, using tables built into the program, it modifies the machine language code so that it will execute properly at its new home. The relocator then jumps to the high memory copy of DOS and the old image is forgotten.

The DOS boot is completed by the DOS coldstart routine. This code initializes DOS, making space for the file buffers, setting HIMEM, building the page 3 vector table, and running the HELLO program.

Previous versions of DOS were somewhat more complicated in the implementation of the bootstrap. In these versions, Boot 1 was loaded at $300 and it, in turn, loaded Boot 2 at $3600, as does version 3.3. Unlike 3.3, however, 27 sectors of DOS were not always loaded. If the diskette was a slave diskette, only 25 sectors were loaded, and, on 13 sector diskettes, this meant the DOS image ended either with sector 8 or sector A of track 2 depending upon whether the diskette was a slave or master. In addition, Boot 1 had a different form of nibbilization (see chapter 3) than any other sector on the diskette, making its raw appearance in memory at $3600 non-executable.

The various stages of the bootstrap process will be covered again in greater detail in Chapter 8, DOS PROGRAM LOGIC.

CHAPTER 6
USING DOS FROM ASSEMBLY LANGUAGE

CAVEAT

This chapter is aimed at the advanced assembly language programmer who wishes to access the disk without resorting to the PRINT statement scheme used with BASIC. Accordingly, the topics covered here may be beyond the comprehension (at least for the present) of a programmer who has never used assembly language.

DIRECT USE OF DISK DRIVE

It is often desirable or necessary to access the Apple's disk drives directly from assembly language, without the use of DOS. This is done using a section of 16 addresses that are latched toggles, interfacing directly to the hardware. There are eight two byte toggles that essentially represent pulling a TTL line high or low. Applications which could use direct disk access range from a user written operating system to DOS-independent utility programs. The device address assignments are given in Figure 6.1.

THIS CHAPTER IS FOR A SELECT GROUP OF PROGRAMMERS.

ADDRESS	LABEL	DESCRIPTION
$C080	PHASEOFF	Stepper motor phase 0 off.
$C081	PHASEON	Stepper motor phase 0 on.
$C082	PHASE1OFF	Stepper motor phase 1 off.
$C083	PHASE1ON	Stepper motor phase 1 on.
$C084	PHASE2OFF	Stepper motor phase 2 off.
$C085	PHASE2ON	Stepper motor phase 2 on.
$C086	PHASE3OFF	Stepper motor phase 3 off.
$C087	PHASE3ON	Stepper motor phase 3 on.
$C088	MOTOROFF	Turn motor off.
$C089	MOTORON	Turn motor on.
$C08A	DRV0EN	Engage drive 1.
$C08B	DRV1EN	Engage drive 2.
$C08C	Q6L	Strobe Data Latch for I/O.
$C08D	Q6H	Load Data Latch.
$C08E	Q7L	Prepare latch for input.
$C08F	Q7H	Prepare latch for output.

Q7L with Q6L = Read
Q7L with Q6H = Sense Write Protect
Q7H with Q6L = Write
Q7H with Q6H = Load Write Latch

FIGURE 6.1 — DOS HARDWARE ADDRESSES

The addresses are slot dependent and the offsets are computed by multiplying the slot number by 16. In hexadecimal this works out nicely and we can add the value $s0 (where s is the slot number) to the base address. If we wanted to engage disk drive number 1 in slot number 6, for example, we would add $60 to $C08A (device address assignment for engaging drive 1) for a result of $C0EA. However, since it is generally desirable to write code that is not slot dependent, one would normally use $C08A,X (where the X register contains the value $s0).

In general, the above addresses need only be accessed with any valid 6502 instruction. However, in the case of reading and writing bytes, care must be taken to insure that the data will be in an appropriate register. All of the following would engage drive number 1. (Assume slot number 6)

```
LDA $C0EA
BIT $C08A,X (where X-reg contains $60)
CMP $C08A,X (where X-reg contains $60)
```

Below are typical examples demonstrating the use of the device address assignments. For more examples, see APPENDIX A. Slot 6 is assumed and the X-register contains $60.

STEPPER PHASE OFF/ON:

Basically, each or the four phases (0-3) must be turned on and then off again. Done in ascending order, this moves the arm inward. In descending order, this moves the arm outward. The timing between accesses to these locations is critical, making this a non-trivial exercise. It is recommended that the SEEK command in RWTS be used to move the arm. See the section on using RWTS immediately following.

MOTOR OFF/ON:

```
        LDA $C088,X     Turn motor off.

        LDA $C089,X     Turn motor on.
```

NOTE: A sufficient delay should be provided to allow the motor time to come up to speed. Shugart recommends one second, but DOS is able to reduce this delay by watching the read latch until data starts to change.

ENGAGE DRIVE 1/2:

```
        LDA $C08A,X     Engage drive 1.

        LDA $C08B,X     Engage drive 2.
```

READ A BYTE:

```
  READ  LDA $C08C,X
        BPL READ
```

NOTE: $C08E,X must already have been accessed to assure Read mode. The loop is necessary to assure that the accumulator will contain valid data. If the data latch does not yet contain valid data the high bit will be zero.

SENSE WRITE PROTECT:

```
        LDA $C08D,X
        LDA $C08E,X     Sense write protect.
        BMI ERROR       If high bit set, protected.
```

WRITE LOAD AND WRITE A BYTE:

```
        LDA DATA
        STA $C08D,X     Write load.
        ORA $C08C,X     Write byte.
```

NOTE: $C08F,X must already have been accessed to insure Write mode and a 100 microsecond delay should be invoked before writing.

Due to hardware constraints, data bytes must be written in 32 cycle loops. Below is an example for an immediate load of the accumulator, followed by a write. Timing is so critical that different routines may be necessary, depending on how the data is to be accessed, and code can not cross memory page boundaries without an adjustment.

```
        LDA #$D5        (2 cycles)
        JSR WRITE9      (6)
        LDA #$AA        (2)
        JSR WRITE9      (6)
        .
        .
        .
WRITE9  CLC             (2)
WRITE7  PHA             (3)
        PLA             (4)
WRITE   STA $C08D,X     (5)
        ORA $C08C,X     (4)
        RTS             (6)
```

CALLING READ/WRITE TRACK/SECTOR (RWTS)

Read/Write Track/Sector (RWTS) exists in every version of DOS as a collection of subroutines, occupying roughly the top third of the DOS program. The interface to RWTS is standardized and thoroughly documented by Apple and may be called by a program running outside of DOS.

There are two subroutines which must be called or whose function must be performed.

JSR $3E3 - When this subroutine is called, the Y and A registers are loaded with the address of the Input/Output control Block (IOB) used by DOS when accessing RWTS. The low order part of the address is in Y and the high order part in A. This subroutine should be called to locate the IOB and the results may be stored in two zero page locations to allow storing values in the IOB and retrieving output values after a call to RWTS. Of course, you may set up your own IOB as long as the Y and A registers point to your IOB upon calling RWTS.

JSR $3D9 - This is the main entry to the RWTS routine. Prior to making this call, the Y and A registers must be loaded with the address of an IOB describing the operation to be performed. This may be done by first calling $3E3 as described above. The IOB must contain appropriate information as defined in the list on the facing page (offsets are given in hexadecimal):

INPUT/OUTPUT CONTROL BLOCK — GENERAL FORMAT

```
BYTE     DESCRIPTION
00       Table type, must be $01
01       Slot number times 16 (s0: s=slot.  Example: $60)
02       Drive number ($01 or $02)
03       Volume number expected ($00 matches any volume)
04       Track number ($00 through $22)
05       Sector number ($00 through $0F)
06-07    Address (LO/HI) of the Device Characteristics Table
08-09    Address (LO/HI) of the 256 byte buffer for
         READ/WRITE
0A       Not used
0B       Byte count for partial sector ($00 for 256 bytes)
0C       Command code     $00 = SEEK
                          $01 = READ
                          $02 = WRITE
                          $04 = FORMAT
0D       Return code - The processor CARRY flag is set upon
                       return from RWTS if there is a
                       non-zero return code:
                          $00 = No errors
                          $08 = Error during initialization
                          $10 = Write protect error
                          $20 = Volume mismatch error
                          $40 = Drive error
                          $80 = Read error (obsolete)
0E       Volume number of last access (must be initialized)
0F       Slot number of last access*16 (must be initialized)
10       Drive number of last access (must be initialized)
```

DEVICE CHARACTERISTICS TABLE

```
BYTE     DESCRIPTION
00       Device type (should be $00 for DISK II)
01       Phases per track (should be $01 for DISK II)
02-03    Motor on time count (should be $EFD8 for DISK II)
```

NOTE: RWTS uses zero-page location $48, which is also used by the APPLE monitor to hold the P-register value. Location $48 should be set to zero after each call to RWTS.

RWTS IOB BY CALL TYPE

```
SEEK     Move disk arm to desired track

Input:   Byte 00    - Table type ($01)
              01    - Slot number * 16 (s0: s=slot)
              02    - Drive number ($01 or $02)
              04    - Track number ($00 through $22)
              06/07 - Pointer to the DCT
              0C    - Command code for SEEK ($00)
              0F    - Slot number of last access * 16
              10    - Drive number of last access

Output: Byte 0D     - Return code (See previous definition)
             0F     - Current Slot number * 16
             10     - Current Drive number
```

```
READ     Read a sector into a specified buffer

Input:   Byte 00    - Table type ($01)
              01    - Slot number * 16 (s0: s=slot)
              02    - Drive number ($01 or $02)
              03    - Volume number ($00 matches any volume)
              04    - Track number ($00 through $22)
              05    - Sector number ($00 through $0F)
              06/07 - Pointer to the DCT
              08/09 - Pointer to 256 byte user data buffer
              0B    - Byte count per sector ($00)
              0C    - Command code for READ ($01)
              0E    - Volume number of last access
              0F    - Slot number of last access * 16
              10    - Drive number of last access

Output: Byte 0D     - Return code (See previous definition)
             0E     - Current Volume number
             0F     - Current Slot number * 16
             10     - Current Drive number
```

```
WRITE    Write a sector from a specified buffer

Input:   Byte 00    - Table type ($01)
              01    - Slot number * 16 (s0: s=slot)
              02    - Drive number ($01 or $02)
              03    - Volume number ($00 matches any volume)
              04    - Track number ($00 through $22)
              05    - Sector number ($00 through $0F)
              06/07 - Pointer to the DCT
              08/09 - Pointer to 256 byte user data buffer
              0B    - Byte count per sector ($00)
              0C    - Command code for WRITE ($02)
              0E    - Volume number of last access
              0F    - Slot number of last access * 16
              10    - Drive number of last access

Output: Byte 0D     - Return code (See previous definition)
             0E     - Current Volume number
             0F     - Current Slot number * 16
             10     - Current Drive number
```

FORMAT Initialize the diskette (does not put DOS on disk, create a VTOC/CATALOG, or store HELLO program)

```
Input:  Byte 00    - Table type ($01)
             01    - Slot number * 16 (s0: s=slot)
             02    - Drive number ($01 or $02)
             03    - Volume number ($00 will default to 254)
             06/07 - Pointer to the DCT
             0C    - Command code for FORMAT ($04)
             0E    - Volume number of last access
             0F    - Slot number of last access * 16
             10    - Drive number of last access

Output: Byte 0D    - Return code (See previous definition)
             0E    - Current Volume number
             0F    - Current Slot number * 16
             10    - Current Drive number
```

CALLING THE DOS FILE MANAGER

The DOS file manager exists in every version of DOS as a collection of subroutines occupying approximately the central third of the DOS program. The interface to these routines is generalized in such a way that they may be called by a program running outside of DOS. The definition of this interface has never been published by APPLE (or anyone else, for that manner) but since the calls can be made through fixed vectors, and, the format of the parameter lists passed have not changed in all the versions of DOS, these routines may be relied upon as "safe". Indeed, the new FID utility program uses these routines to process files on the diskette.

There are two subroutines which must be called in order to access the file manager.

JSR $3DC - When this subroutine is called, the Y and A registers are loaded with the address of the file manager parameter list. The low order part of the address is in Y and the high order part in A. This subroutine must be called at least once to locate this parameter list and the results may be stored in two zero page locations to allow the programmer to set input values in the parameter list and to locate output values there after file manager calls.

JSR $3D6 - This is the main entry to the file manager. Prior to making this call the parameter list, located using the call described above, must be completed appropriately, depending upon the type of call, and the X register must be set to either zero or non-zero as follows:

```
X = 0 - If file is not found, allocate it
X # 0 - If file is not found, do not allocate one
```

Normally, X should be zero on an OPEN call for a new file and non-zero for all other call types.

Three buffers must be provided to the file manager by the programmer, allocated by him in his memory. These buffers, together, occupy 557 bytes of RAM, and must be passed to the file manager each time their associated file is used. A separate set of these buffers must be maintained for each open file. DOS maintains buffers for this purpose, as described in earlier chapters, in high RAM. These buffers may be "borrowed" from DOS if care is taken to let DOS know about it. A method for doing this will be outlined later.

A chart giving the required inputs for each call type to the file manager is given in Figure 6.2. The general format of the file manager parameter list is as follows:

FILE MANAGER PARAMETER LIST — GENERAL FORMAT

```
BYTE   DESCRIPTION
00     Call type: 01=OPEN         05=DELETE          09=RENAME
                  02=CLOSE        06=CATALOG         0A=POSITION
                  03=READ         07=LOCK            0B=INIT
                  04=WRITE        08=UNLOCK          0C=VERIFY
01     Sub-call type for READ or WRITE:
                  00=No operation (ignore call entirely)
                  01=READ or WRITE one byte
                  02=READ or WRITE a range of bytes
                  03=POSITION then READ or WRITE one byte
                  04=POSITION then READ/WRITE a range
02-09  Parameters specific to the call type used. See
       FILE MANAGER PARAMETER LIST BY CALL TYPE below.
0A     Return code (note: not all return codes can occur
                  for any call type). The processor CARRY
                  flag is set upon return from the file
                  manager if there is a non-zero return code:
                  00=No errors
                  01=Not used ("LANGUAGE NOT AVAILABLE")
                  02=Bad call type
                  03=Bad sub-call type (greater than four)
                  04=WRITE PROTECTED
                  05=END OF DATA
                  06=FILE NOT FOUND (was allocated if X=0)
                  07=VOLUME MISMATCH
                  08=DISK I/O ERROR
                  09=DISK FULL
                  0A=FILE LOCKED
0B     Not used
0C-0D  Address of a 45 byte buffer which will be used by the
       file manager to save its status between calls. This
       area is called the file manager workarea and need not
       be initialized by the caller but the space must be
       provided and this two byte address field initialized.
       (addresses are in low/high order format)
0E-0F  Address of a 256 byte buffer which will be used by the
       file manager to maintain the current Track/Sector List
       sector for the open file. Buffer itself need not be
       initialized by the caller.
10-11  Address of a 256 byte buffer which will be used by the
       file manager to maintain the data sector buffer.
       Buffer need not be initialized by the caller.
```

	00	01	02	03	04	05	06	07	08	09	0A	0B	0C	0D	0E	0F	10	11
OPEN	01		RECORD LENGTH OR 0000		V	D	S	FILE TYPE	FILE NAME ADDRESS		RETURN CODE (OUTPUT)		ADDR. OF FILE MANAGER WORK AREA BUFFER		ADDR. OF T/S LIST BUFFER			
CLOSE	02																DATA SECTOR BUFFER ADDRESS	
READ	03	SUBCODE	RECORD NUMBER		BYTE OFFSET		RANGE LENGTH		ONE DATA BYTE	RANGE ADDR.								
WRITE	04																	
DELETE	05				V	D	S		FILE NAME ADDRESS									
CATALOG	06					D	S											
LOCK	07				V	D	S		FILE NAME ADDRESS						T/S LIST ADDRESS			
UNLOCK	08				V	D	S											
RENAME	09		NEW NAME ADDRESS		V	D	S											
POSITION	0A		RECORD NUMBER		BYTE OFFSET													
INIT	0B	DOS PAGE NO.			V	D	S											
VERIFY	0C				V	D	S		FILE NAME ADDRESS						T/S LIST ADDRESS		DATA BUFF. ADDRESS	

FIGURE 6.2 — FILE MANAGER PARAMETER LIST REQUIRED INPUT

CALLING THE FILE MANAGER

FILE MANAGER PARAMETER LIST BY CALL TYPE

```
OPEN     Locates or creates a file. A call to POSITION should
         follow every OPEN.

Input:   Byte 00    - 01
              02/03 - Fixed record length or 0000 if variable
              04    - Volume number or 00 for any volume
              05    - Drive number to be used (01 or 02)
              06    - Slot number to be used (01-07)
              07    - File type (used only for new files)
                      $00 = TEXT
                      $01 = INTEGER BASIC
                      $02 = APPLESOFT BASIC
                      $04 = BINARY
                      $08 = S TYPE FILE
                      $10 = RELOCATABLE
                      $20 = A TYPE FILE
                      $40 = B TYPE FILE
              08/09 - Address of file name (30 characters)
                      (Low/high format)
              0C/0D - Address of file manager workarea buffer
              0E/0F - Address of T/S List sector buffer
              10/11 - Address of data sector buffer

Output:  Byte 07    - File type of file which was OPENed
              0A    - Return code (see previous definitions)
```

```
CLOSE    Write out final sectors, update the Catalog.
         A CLOSE call is required eventually for every OPEN.

Input:   Byte 00    - 02
              0C/0D - Address of file manager workarea buffer
              0E/0F - Address of T/S List sector buffer
              10/11 - Address of data sector buffer

Output:  Byte 0A    - Return code
```

```
READ     Read one or a range of bytes from the file to memory.
WRITE    Write one or a range of bytes from memory to the file.

Input:   Byte 00    - 03 (READ) 04 (WRITE)
              01    - Subcode:
                      00 = No operation
                      01 = READ or WRITE one byte only
                      02 = READ or WRITE a range of bytes
                      03 = POSITION then READ/WRITE one byte
                      04 = POSITION then READ/WRITE range
              02/03 - (Subcodes 03 or 04) Record number
              04/05 - (Subcodes 03 or 04) Byte offset
              06/07 - (Subcodes 02 or 04) Number of bytes in
                      range to be read or written. (Note: for
                      WRITE, this length must be one less
                      than the actual length to be written)
```

```
              08/09 - (Subcodes 02 or 04) Address of range of
                      bytes to be written or address of
                      buffer to which bytes are to be read.
              08    - (WRITE, Subcodes 01 or 03) Single byte
                      to be written.
              0C/0D - Address of file manager workarea buffer
              0E/0F - Address of T/S List sector buffer
              10/11 - Address of data sector buffer

Output: Byte  02/03 - Record number of current file position
              04/05 - Byte offset of current file position*
              08    - (READ, Subcodes 01 or 03) Byte read
              0A    - Return code
```

*The current file position is updated to point to the byte following the data read or written.

```
DELETE  Locate and delete a file, freeing its sectors.

Input:  Byte 00    - 05
             (remainder are the same as with OPEN call type)

Output: Byte 0A    - Return code
```

```
CATALOG Produce a catalog listing on the output device.

Input:  Byte 00    - 06
             05    - Drive
             06    - Slot
             0C/0D - Address of file manager workarea buffer

Output: Byte 0A    - Return code
```

```
LOCK    Lock a file.

Input:  Byte 00    - 07
             (remainder are the same as with OPEN call type)

Output: Byte 0A    - Return code
```

```
UNLOCK  Unlock a file.

Input:  Byte 00    - 08
             (remainder are the same as with OPEN call type)

Output: Byte 0A    - Return code
```

```
RENAME  Rename a file.

Input:  Byte 00    - 09
             02/03 - Address of new file name (30 bytes)
             (remainder are the same as with OPEN call type)

Output: Byte 0A    - Return code
```

```
POSITION Calculate the location of a record and/or byte
         offset in the file. Position such that next READ or
         WRITE will be at that location in the file. A call
         to POSITION (either explicitly or implictly using
         subcodes of READ or WRITE) is required prior to the
         first READ or WRITE. Bytes 02 through 05 should be
         set to zeros for a normal position to the beginning
         of the file.

Input:   Byte 00    - 0A
              02/03 - Relative record number for files with a
                      fixed length record size or zero. First
                      record of file is record 0000.
              04/05 - Relative byte offset into record or of
                      entire file if record number is zero.
              0C/0D - Address of file manager workarea buffer.

Output:  Byte 0A    - Return code
```

```
INIT     Initialize a slave diskette. This function formats a
         diskette and writes a copy of DOS onto tracks 0-2.
         A VTOC and Catalog are also created.  A HELLO program
         is not stored, however.

Input:   Byte 00    - 0B
              01    - First page of DOS image to be copied to
                      the diskette. Normally $9D for a 48K
                      machine.
              04    - Volume number of new diskette.
              05    - Drive number (01 or 02)
              06    - Slot number (01-07)
              0C/0D - Address of file manager workarea buffer.

Output:  Byte 0A    - Return code
```

```
VERIFY   Verify that there are no bad sectors in a file by
         reading every sector.

Input:   Byte 00    - 0C
              (remainder are the same as the OPEN call type)

Output:  Byte 0A    - Return code
```

DOS BUFFERS

Usually it is desirable to use one of DOS's buffers when calling the file manager to save memory. DOS buffers consist of each of the three buffers used by the file manager (file manager workarea, T/S List sector, and data sector) as well as a 30 byte file name buffer and some link pointers. All together a DOS buffer occupies 595 bytes of memory. The address of the first DOS buffer is stored in the first two bytes of DOS ($9D00 on a 48K APPLE II). The address of the next buffer is stored in the first and so on in a chain of linked elements. The link address to the next buffer in the last buffer is zeros. If the buffer is not being used by DOS, the first byte of the file name field is a hex 00. Otherwise, it contains the first character of the name of the open file. The assembly language programmer should follow these conventions to avoid having DOS reuse the buffer while he is using it. This means that the name of the file should be stored in the buffer to reserve it for exclusive use (or at least a non-zero byte stored on the first character) and later, when the user is through with the buffer, a 00 should be stored on the file name to return it to DOS's use. If the later is not done, DOS will eventually run out of available buffers and will refuse even to do a CATALOG command. A diagram of the DOS buffers for MAXFILES 3 is given in Figure 6.3 and the format of a DOS buffer is given below.

DOS BUFFER FORMAT

BYTE	DESCRIPTION
000/0FF	Data sector buffer (256 bytes in length)
100/1FF	T/S List sector buffer (256 bytes in length)
200/22C	File manager workarea buffer (45 bytes in length)
22D/24A	File name buffer (30 bytes in length) First byte indicates whether this DOS buffer is being used. If hex 00, buffer is free for use.
24B/24C	Address (Lo/High) of file manager workarea buffer
24D/24E	Address of T/S List sector buffer
24F/250	Address of data sector buffer
251/252	Address of the file name field of the next buffer on the chain of buffers. If this is the last buffer on the chain then this field contains zeros.

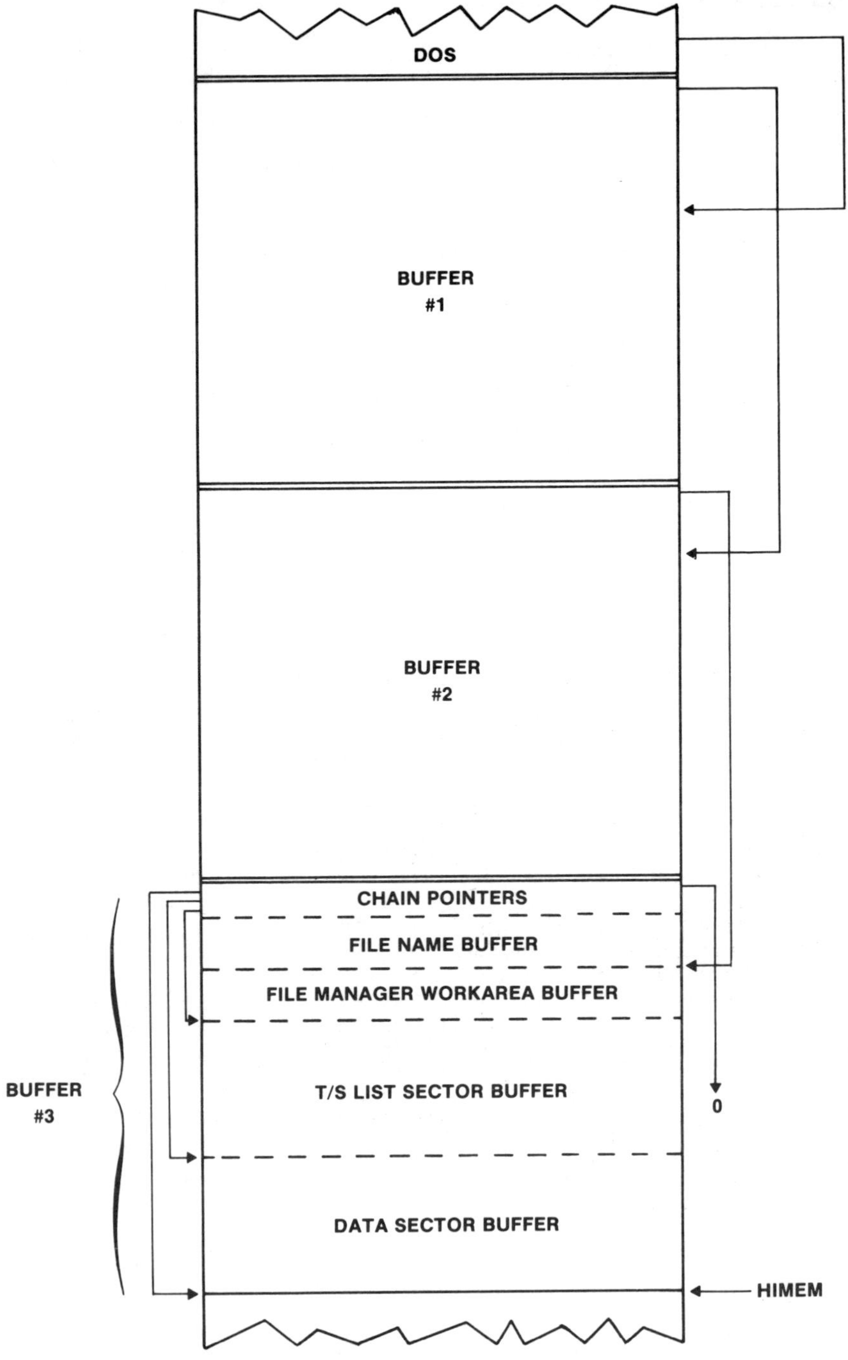

FIGURE 6.3 — DOS FILE BUFFERS

THE FILE MANAGER WORKAREA

The file manager workarea contains the variables which, taken together, constitute all of the information the file manager needs to deal with an open file. Each time the file manager finishes processing a call, it copies all of its important variables into the file manager workarea buffer provided by the caller. Each subsequent time the file manager is called, the first thing it does is to copy the contents of the file manager workarea buffer back into its variables so that it may resume processing for the file where it left off on the previous call. Ordinarily, the programmer will have no need to worry about the contents of this workarea, since most of the useful information is present in the parameter list anyway. Occasionally, it is handy to know more about the open file. For these cases, the format of the file manager workarea is given below:

FILE MANAGER WORKAREA FORMAT

BYTE	DESCRIPTION
00/01	Track/Sector of first T/S List for file
02/03	Track/Sector of current T/S List for file
04	Flags: 80=T/S List buffer changed and needs writing 40=Data buffer has been changed and needs writing 02=Volume freespace map changed and needs writing
05/06	Track/Sector of current data sector
07	Sector offset into catalog to entry for this file
08	Byte offset into catalog sector to entry for file
09/0A	Maximum data sectors represented by one T/S List
0B/0C	Offset of first sector in current T/S List
0D/0E	Offset of last sector in current T/S List
0F/10	Relative sector number last read
11/12	Sector size in bytes (256)
13/14	Current position in sectors (relative)
15	Current byte offset in this sector
16	Not used
17/18	Fixed record length
19/1A	Current record number
1B/1C	Byte offset into current record
1D/1E	Length of file in sectors
1F	Next sector to allocate on this track
20	Current track being allocated
21/24	Bit map of available sectors on this track (rotated)
25	File type (80=locked) 0,1,2,4=T,I,A,B
26	Slot number times 16 (example: $60=slot 6)
27	Drive number (01 or 02)
28	Volume number (complemented)
29	Track
2A/2C	Not used

COMMON ALGORITHMS

Given below are several pieces of code which are used when working with DOS:

LOCATE A FREE DOS BUFFER

The following subroutine may be used to locate an unallocated DOS buffer for use with the DOS file manager.

```
FBUFF    LDA    $3D2     LOCATE DOS LOAD POINT
         STA    $1
         LDY    #0
         STY    $0
*
GBUF0    LDA    ($0),Y   LOCATE NEXT DOS BUFFER
         PHA
         INY
         LDA    ($0),Y
         STA    $1
         PLA
         STA    $0
         BNE    GBUF     GOT ONE
         LDA    $1
         BEQ    NBUF     NO BUFFERS FREE
*
GBUF     LDY    #0       GET FILENAME
         LDA    ($0),Y
         BEQ    GOTBUF   ITS FREE
         LDY    #36      ITS NOT FREE
         BNE    GBUF0    GO GET NEXT BUFFER
*
GOTBUF   CLC             INDICATE-GOT A FREE BUFFER
         RTS             RETURN TO CALLER
NBUF     SEC             INDICATE-NO FREE BUFFERS
         RTS             RETURN TO CALLER
```

WHICH VERSION OF DOS IS ACTIVE?

In case the program has version dependent code, a check of the DOS version may be required:

```
         CLC
         LDA    #0       ADD $16BE TO DOS LOAD POINT
         ADC    #$BE
         STA    $0
         LDA    $3D2
         ADC    #$16
         STA    $1
         LDY    #0
         LDA    ($0),Y   GET DOS VERSION NUMBER (2 OR 3)
```

IS DOS IN THE MACHINE?

The following series of instructions should be used prior to attempting to call RWTS or the file manager to insure that DOS is present on this machine.

```
        LDA     $3D0     GET VECTOR JMP
        CMP     #$4C     IS IT A JUMP?
        BNE     NODOS    NO, DOS NOT LOADED
```

WHICH BASIC IS SELECTED?

Some programs depend upon either the INTEGER BASIC ROM or the APPLESOFT ROM. To find out which is active and select the one desired, the following subroutine can be called. First the A register is loaded with a code to indicate which BASIC is desired. $20 is used for INTEGER BASIC and $4C is used for APPLESOFT. To set up for APPLESOFT, for example:

```
        LDA     #$4C     CODE FOR APPLESOFT
        JSR     SETBSC   CALL SUBROUTINE
        BNE     ERROR    LANGUAGE NOT AVAILABLE
        .
        .
        .
SETBSC  CMP     $E000    CORRECT BASIC ALREADY THERE?
        BEQ     RTS      YES
        STA     $C080    NO, SELECT ROM CARD
        CMP     $E000    NOW DO WE HAVE IT?
        BEQ     RTS      YES
        STA     $C081    NO, TRY ROM CARD OUT
        CMP     $E000    GOT IT NOW?
RTS     RTS              IN ANY CASE, EXIT TO CALLER
```

SEE IF A BASIC PROGRAM IS IN EXECUTION

To determine if there is a BASIC program running or if BASIC is in immediate command mode, use the following statements:

```
 ..IF INTEGER BASIC IS ACTIVE...
        LDA     $D9
        BMI     EXEC     PROGRAM EXECUTING
        BPL     NOEXEC   PROGRAM NOT EXECUTING

 ..IF APPLESOFT BASIC IS ACTIVE...
        LDX     $76      GET LINE NUMBER
        INX
        BEQ     NOEXEC   PROGRAM NOT EXECUTING
        LDX     $33      GET PROMPT CHARACTER
        CPX     #$DD     PROMPT IS A "]"?
        BEQ     NOEXEC   YES, NOT EXECUTING
        BNE     EXEC     ELSE, PROGRAM IS EXECUTING
```

CHAPTER 7
CUSTOMIZING DOS

Although DOS usually provides most of the functionality needed by the BASIC or assembly language programmer, at times a custom change is required. Making changes to your copy of DOS should only be undertaken when absolutely necessary, since new versions of DOS are released from time to time, and the job of moving several patches to a new version of DOS every few months can become a burden. In addition, wholesale modification of DOS without a clear understanding of the full implications of each change can result in an unreliable system.

SLAVE VS MASTER PATCHING

The usual procedure for making changes to DOS involves "patching" the object or machine language code in DOS. Once a desired change is identified, a few instructions are stored over other instructions within DOS to modify the program. There are three levels at which changes to DOS may be applied.

1 - A patch can be made to the DOS in memory. If this is done, a later reboot will cause the change to "fall out" or be removed.

2 - A patch of the first type can be made permanent by initializing a diskette while running the patched DOS. This procedure creates a slave diskette with a copy of DOS on tracks 0, 1, and 2 which contains the patch. Each time this newly created diskette is booted the patched version of DOS will be loaded. Also, any slave diskettes created by that diskette will also contain the patched version of DOS.

3 - The patch is applied directly to a master diskette. This is somewhat more complicated. Either the patch may be made to the image of DOS on the first three tracks of a master diskette using a zap program, or MASTER CREATE may be used to write the changed copy of DOS to a new diskette. The following procedure may be followed to do this:

```
BLOAD MASTER CREATE
Get into the monitor (CALL -151)
Store a $4C at location $80D (80D:4C)
Execute MASTER CREATE (800G)
```

When MASTER CREATE finishes loading the DOS image it will exit. You may use the monitor to make changes in the image. MASTER CREATE loads DOS into memory at $1200 such that Boot 2 (RWTS) is loaded first, followed by the main part of DOS starting at $1C00.

When all patches have been made, reenter MASTER CREATE at location $82D (82DG).

Complete the MASTER CREATE update normally. The resulting diskette will have the patches applied.

This procedure will work for versions 3.2, 3.2.1, and 3.3 of DOS.

CUSTOMIZING DOS

AVOIDING RELOAD OF LANGUAGE CARD

A rather annoying addition to DOS 3.3 was a patch to the Boot 2 code to store a binary zero in the first byte of the language card, forcing DOS to reload BASIC (either INTEGER or APPLESOFT) for every boot, whether or not the machine was just powered up. When the machine is first powered up this patch is not necessary, because the first byte of the language card does not appear to DOS to be either BASIC, and the card will always be loaded. On subsequent reboots, more often than not a good copy of BASIC already resides in the language card and this patch results in a LANGUAGE NOT AVAILABLE error message after booting a slave diskette. Presumably the patch was added to version 3.3 to allow for the possibility that a future language might have a first byte of code that matched one of the BASICs, thus confusing DOS and causing unknown results. If the user always powers the machine off and on when switching from DOS to some other operating system (i.e., PASCAL or CP/M), the patch may be removed as follows.

At $BFD3 (48K) is a STA instruction which stores a zero on the language card. This instruction must be changed to three no-operation instructions:

```
BFD3:EA EA EA
```

A slave diskette may then be INITed using this modified version of DOS and that diskette will not reload BASIC when booted. A master diskette may be patched in this manner and will create the desired result on an original Apple or an Apple IIe. In the case of an Apple II Plus, however, the HELLO file on a master diskette will always reload the language card anyway.

INSERTING A PROGRAM BETWEEN DOS AND ITS BUFFERS

Once in a while it is useful to find a "safe" place to load a machine language program (a printer driver, perhaps) where BASIC and DOS can never walk over it, even if DOS is coldstarted. If the program is less than 200 bytes long, $300 is a good choice. For larger programs, it is usually better to "tuck" the program in between DOS and its buffers (assuming the program is relocatable and will run at that location). To do this, load the program into low RAM, copy it to high RAM right below $9D00 (for a 48K machine), over the top of DOS's buffers, change the first buffer address at $9D00 to point below your program, (remember to allow 38 extra bytes for the filename and link fields) and JMP to $3D3 (DOS COLDSTART). This will cause DOS to rebuild its buffers below your program and "forget" about the memory your program occupies until the next time DOS is booted. Of course, BASIC can not get at that memory either, since its HIMEM is below the DOS buffers.

BRUN OR EXEC THE HELLO FILE

Ordinarily, when DOS finishes booting into memory, it performs a RUN command on the HELLO file in its file name buffer (left there by the INIT command which wrote DOS to the diskette). To change the RUN command to a BRUN or an EXEC, apply the following patch to DOS (48K):

```
9E42:34 (for BRUN) ..or.. 9E42:14 (for EXEC)
```

REMOVING THE PAUSE DURING A LONG CATALOG

Normally, when a CATALOG command is done on a disk with many files, DOS will pause every time the screen fills with names to allow the user time to see them all. By pressing any key the CATALOG continues. If this pause is undesirable, apply the following patch to DOS (48K):

```
AE34:60
```

CHANGING THE HELLO FILE NAME

You can change the name of the HELLO file by changing the contents of DOS's primary file name buffer. For example, to change the primary file name from HELLO to HI THERE, the patch is (48K):

```
AA75:C8 C9 A0 D4 C8 C5 D2 C5
```

PUT CURSOR ON COMMAND THAT CAUSED DOS ERROR

When you get a DOS error message such as "FILE NOT FOUND" or "FILE TYPE MISMATCH" because you typed the wrong file name or misspelled it slightly, it would be nice if DOS would return the cursor to the line with your faulty command so you could more easily retype it. To make DOS do this from now on, apply the following patches (48K).

```
     A6FF:4C DF BC (was 6C 5E 9D)
       and
     BCDF:C6 25 C6 25 C6 25 C6 25 20 22 FC 6C 5E 9D
```

This patch causes a jump to some new logic at $BCDF, an unused area of RWTS.

ALLOW THE VALUE OF THE L KEYWORD OF A BSAVE TO EXCEED 32K

This patch allows you to save more than 32K with the BSAVE command. It simply involves changing one byte from 7F to FF. Apply the following patch (48K):

```
     A964:FF
```

UPDATING PRE-1983 DOS 3.3

Minor revisions to DOS 3.3 were made in early January, 1983. These revisions are explained on pages 2-4 and 8-41. If you have an earlier version of DOS 3.3 and wish to update it to the latest version, poke in these changes and then save DOS using method 2 or 3 on page 7-1. The following changes are for a 48K system.

```
A6BB:20 69 BA

B33E:18 AD BF B5 8D EC B5 6D E6 B5 8D E6 B5 AD C0 B5
    :8D ED B5 6D E4 B5 8D E4 B5 90 03 EE E5 B5 60 00 00

B684:84 BA

B6AA:BB

BA69:AE 5F AA E0 1C F0 05 A2 00 8E 5D B6 60 A9 FF 8D
    :FB 04 8D 0C C0 8D 0E C0 4C 2F FB AD BD B5 8D E6
    :B5 8D EA B5 BA 8E 9B B3 4C 7F 00 00

BFD6:20 76 BA 4C 44 B7
```

CHAPTER 8
DOS PROGRAM LOGIC

This chapter will take a detailed look at the operation of the DOS program itself to aid the APPLE user in understanding it and to help him to make intelligent use of its facilities. Each subroutine and group of variables or constants will be covered separately by storage address. The enterprising programmer may wish to create a disassembly of DOS on his printer and transfer the annotations given here directly to such a listing. Addresses used will be for DOS 3.3 and for a 48K master diskette version of DOS. Slot 6 is assumed. Unless specifically indicated by a $ character, lengths are given in decimal, addresses in hexadecimal (base 16).

DISK II CONTROLLER CARD ROM — BOOT 0

ADDRESS	
C600-C65B	This routine is the first code executed when a disk is to be booted. It receives control via PR#6 or C600G or 6 control-P. Dynamically build a translate table for converting disk codes to six bit hex at location $356-$3FF. Call an RTS instruction in the monitor ROM and extract the return address from the stack to find out the address of this controller card ROM. Use this address to determine the slot number of this drive by shifting $Csxx. Save the slot number times 16 ($s0) Clear disk I/O latches, set read mode, select drive 1, turn disk drive on. Pull disk arm back over 80 tracks to recalibrate the arm to track zero. Set up parms to read sector zero on track zero to location $800. Execution falls through into a general sector read subroutine at C65C.
C65C-C6FA	This subroutine reads the sector number stored at $3D on the track indicated by $41 to the address stored at $26,$27. Look for D5/AA/96 sector address header on the disk. If D5/AA/AD is found and sector data was wanted, go to C6A6.

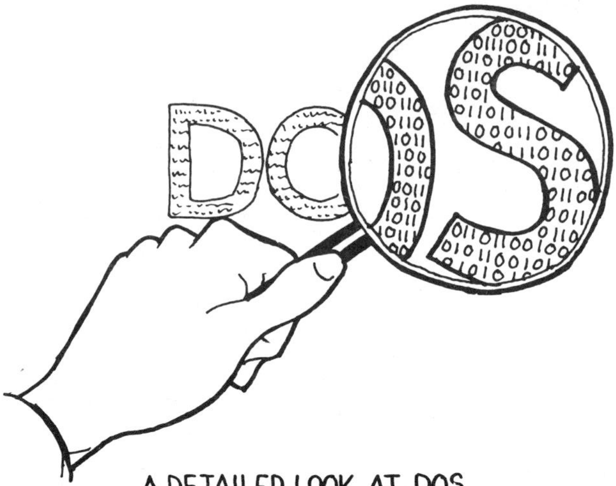

A DETAILED LOOK AT DOS

C683 Handle a sector address block.
Read three double bytes from the disk and combine them to obtain the volume, track, and sector number of the sector being read from the disk at this time.
Store the track at $40.
Compare the sector found to the sector wanted and the track found to the track wanted.
If no match, go back to C65C.
Otherwise, if sector is correct, go to C65D to find the sector data itself.

C6A6 Handle sector data block.
Read the 85 bytes of secondary data to $300-$355.
Read 256 bytes of primary data to the address stored at $26,$27.
Verify that the data checksum is valid.
If not, start over at C65C.
"Nibbilize" the primary and secondary data together into the primary data buffer ($26,$27).
Increment $27 (address page of read data) and $3D (sector number to be read) and check against $800 to see if additional sectors need to be read.
If so, reload slot*16 and go back to C65C to read next sector. (This feature is not used when loading DOS but is used when loading from a BASICS diskette.)
Otherwise, go to $801 to begin executing the second stage of the bootstrap.

FIRST RAM BOOTSTRAP LOADER — BOOT 1

ADDRESS

0801-084C This routine loads the second RAM loader, Boot 2, including RWTS, into memory and jumps to it.
If this is not the first entry to Boot 1, go to $81F.
Get slot*16 and shift down to slot number.
Create the address of the ROM sector read subroutine (C65C in our case) and store it at $3E,$3F.
Pick up the first memory page in which to read Boot 2 from location $8FE, add the length of Boot 2 in sectors from $8FF, and set that value as the first address to which to read (read last page first).

081F Get sector to read, if zero, go to $839.
Translate theoretical sector number into physical sector number by indexing into skewing table at $84D.
Decrement theoretical sector number (8FF) for next iteration through.
Set up parameters for ROM subroutine (C65C) and jump to it. It will return to $801 when the sector has been read.

0839 Adjust page number at 8FE to locate entry point of Boot 2.
Perform a PR#0 and IN#0 by calling the monitor.
Initialize the monitor (TEXT mode, standard window, etc.)
Get slot*16 again and go to Boot 2 ($3700 for a master disk, $B700 in its final relocated location).

DOS 3.3 MAIN ROUTINES

ADDRESS

9D00-9D0F Relocatable address constants

9D00 Address of first DOS buffer at its file name field.
9D02 Address of the DOS keyboard intercept routine.
9D04 Address of the DOS video intercept routine.
9D06 Address of the primary file name buffer.
9D08 Address of the secondary (RENAME) file name buffer.
9D0A Address of the range length parameter used for LOAD.
9D0C Address of the DOS load address ($9D00).
9D0E Address of the file manager parameter list.

9D10-9D1C DOS video (CSWL) intercept's state handler address table. States are used to drive the handling of DOS commands as they appear as output of PRINT statements and this table contains the address of the routine which handles each state from state 0 to state 6.

9D1E-9D55 Command handler entry point table. This table contains the address of a command handler subroutine for each DOS command in the following standard order:

INIT	A54F
LOAD	A413
SAVE	A397
RUN	A4D1
CHAIN	A4F0
DELETE	A263
LOCK	A271
UNLOCK	A275
CLOSE	A2EA
READ	A51B
EXEC	A5C6
WRITE	A510
POSITION	A5DD
OPEN	A2A3
APPEND	A298
RENAME	A281
CATALOG	A56E
MON	A233
NOMON	A23D
PR#	A229
IN#	A22E
MAXFILES	A251
FP	A57A
INT	A59E
BSAVE	A331
BLOAD	A35D
BRUN	A38E
VERIFY	A27D

9D56-9D61 Active BASIC entry point vector table. The addresses stored here are maintained by DOS such that they apply to the current version of BASIC running.

9D56 Address of CHAIN entry point to BASIC.
9D58 Address of RUN.
9D5A Address of error handler.
9D5C Address of BASIC coldstart.
9D5E Address of BASIC warmstart.
9D60 Address of BASIC relocate (APPLESOFT only).

9D62-9D6B Image of the entry point vector for INTEGER BASIC. This image is copied to 9D56 if INTEGER BASIC is made active.

9D6C-9D77 Image of the entry point vector for the ROM version of APPLESOFT.

9D78-9D83 Image of the entry point vector for the RAM version of APPLESOFT.

9D84-9DBE DOS coldstart entry routine.
Get the slot and drive numbers and store as default values for command keywords.
Copy APPLESOFT ROM or INTEGER BASIC entry point vector into current BASIC entry point vector.
Remember which BASIC is active.
Go to 9DD1.

9DBF-9DE9 DOS warmstart entry routine.
Get the remembered BASIC type and set the ROM card as necessary (calls A5B2).
9DD1 Remember whether entry is coldstart or warmstart
Call A851 to replace DOS keyboard and video intercepts.
Set NOMON C,I,O.
Set video intercept handler state to 0.
Coldstart or warmstart the current BASIC (exit DOS).
(DOS will next gain control when BASIC prints its input prompt character)

9DEA-9E50 First entry processing for DOS. This routine is called by the keyboard intercept handler when the first keyboard input request is made by BASIC after a DOS coldstart.
If RAM APPLESOFT is active, copy its entry point vector to the active BASIC entry point vector and blank out the primary file name buffer so that no HELLO file will be run.
Set MAXFILES to 3 by default.
Call A7D4 to build the DOS file buffers.
If an EXEC was active, close the EXEC file
Set the video intercept state to 0 and indicate warmstart status by calling A75B.
If the last command executed was not INIT (this DOS was not just booted), go to 9E45.
Otherwise, copy an image of the DOS jump vector to $3D0-$3FF.
Point $3F2,$3F3 to DOS warmstart routine.
Set the AUTOSTART ROM power-up byte since the RESET handler address was changed.
Set the command index for RUN (to run the HELLO file) and go to A180 to execute it.
9E45 See if there is a pending command.
If so, go to A180 to execute it. Otherwise, return to caller.

9E51-9E7F An image of the DOS page 3 jump vector which the above routine copies to $3D0-$3FF. See Chapter 5 for a description of its contents.

9E81-9EB9 DOS keyboard intercept routine.
Call 9ED1 to save the registers at entry to DOS.
If not coldstarting or reading a disk file, go to 9E9E.
Get value in A register at entry and echo it on the screen (erases flashing cursor).
If in read state (reading a file) go to A626 to get next byte from disk file.
Otherwise, call 9DEA to do first entry processing.
Put cursor on screen in next position.
9E9E If EXECing, call A682 to get the next byte from the EXEC file.
Set the video intercept state to 3 (input echo).
Call 9FBA to restore the registers at entry to DOS.
Call the true keyboard input routine.
Save the input character so that it will be restored with the registers in the A register.
Do the same with the new X register value.
Exit DOS via 9FB3.

9EBA-9EBC A jump to the true KSWL handler routine.

9EBD-9ED0 DOS video intercept routine.
Call 9ED1 to save the registers at entry to DOS.
Get the video intercept state and, using it as an index into the state handler table (9D10), go to the proper handler routine, passing it the character being printed.

9ED1-9EEA Common intercept save registers routine.
Save the A, X, Y, and S registers at AA59-AA5C.
While in DOS, restore the true I/O handlers (KSWL and CSWL) to \$36-\$39.
Return to caller.

9EEB-9F11 State 0 output handler. --start of line--
If a RUN command was interrupted (by loading RAM APPLESOFT) go to 9F78 to complete it.
If read flag is on (file being read) and output is a "?" character (BASIC INPUT), go to state 6 to skip it.
If read flag is on and output is prompt character (\$33) go to state 2 to ignore the line.
Set state to 2 (ignore non-DOS command) just in case.
If output character is not a control-D, go to state 2.
Otherwise, set state to 1 (collect possible DOS command), set line index to zero, and fall through to state 1.

9F12-9F22 State 1 output handler. --collect DOS command--
Using line index, store character in input buffer at \$200.
Increment line index.
If character is not a carriage return, exit DOS via 9F95 (echo character on screen if MON I).
Otherwise, go to command scanner at 9FCD.

9F23-9F2E State 2 output handler. --non-DOS command ignore--
If the character is not a carriage return, exit DOS via 9FA4 (echo character on screen).
Otherwise, set state back to 0 and exit DOS via 9FA4.

9F2F-9F51 State 3 output handler. --INPUT statement handler--
Set state to 0 in case INPUT ends.
If character is not a carriage return, echo it on screen as long as EXEC is not in effect with NOMON I but exit DOS in any case. (KSWL will set state=3)
Otherwise, call A65E to see if BASIC is executing a program or is in immediate mode. If EXEC is running or if BASIC is in immediate mode, go to state 1 to collect the possible DOS command.
Otherwise, exit DOS, echoing the character as appropriate.

9F52-9F60 State 4 output handler. --WRITE data to a file--
If the character is a carriage return, set state to 5 (start of write data line).
Call A60E to write the byte to the disk file.
Exit DOS with echo on screen if MON O.

9F61-9F70 State 5 output handler. --Start of WRITE data line--
If the character is a control-D, go to state 0 to immediately exit write mode.
If the character is a line feed, write it and exit, staying in state 5.
Otherwise, set the state to 4 and go to state 4.

9F71-9F77 State 6 output handler. --Skip prompt character--
Set state to 0.
Exit DOS via 9F9D (echo if MON I).

9F78-9F82 Finish RUN command, interrupted by APPLESOFT RAM LOAD
Reset the "RUN interrupted" flag.
Call A851 to replace the DOS CSWL/KSWL intercepts.
Go to A4DC to complete the RUN command.

9F83-9F94 DOS command scanner exit to BASIC routine.
If first character of command line is control-D, go to echo exit (9F95).
Otherwise, set things up so BASIC won't see the DOS command by passing a zero length line (only a carriage return). Fall through to echo exit.

9F95-9FB0 Echo character on screen (conditionally) and exit DOS
9F95 Echo only if MON C set, otherwise, go to 9FB3.
9F99 Echo only if MON O set, otherwise, go to 9FB3.
9F9D Echo only if MON I set, otherwise, go to 9FB3.
9FA4 Always echo character.
Call 9FBA to restore registers at entry to DOS.
Call 9FC5 to echo character on screen.
Save contents of the registers after echoing.
Fall through to DOS exit routine.

9FB3-9FC4 DOS exit routine and register restore.
Call A851 to put back DOS KSWL/CSWL intercepts.
Restore S (stack) register from entry to DOS.
9FBA DOS register restore subroutine.
Restore registers from first entry to DOS and return to caller.

9FC5-9FC7 A jump to the true CSWL routine.

9FC8-9FCC Skip a line on the screen.
Load a carriage return into the A register and call 9FC5 to print it.

9FCD-A179 DOS command parse routine.
Set the command index to -1 (none).
Reset the pending command flag (none pending).
9FD6 Add one to command index.
If first charcater is a control-D, skip it.
Flush to a non-blank (call A1A4).
Compare command to command name in command name table at A884 for the current command index.
If it doesn't match and if there are more entries left to check, go back to 9FD6.
If it does match, go to A01B.

```
     Otherwise, if command was not found in the table,
     check to see if the first character was a control-D.
     If so, go to A6C4 to print "SYNTAX ERROR".
     Otherwise, call A75B to reset the state and warmstart
     flag and go to 9F95 to echo the command and exit.
     (the command must be for BASIC, not DOS)
A01B Compute an index into the operand table for the
     command which was entered.
     Call A65E to see if a BASIC program is executing.
     If not, and the command is not a direct type command,
     (according to the operand table) go to A6D2 to print
     "NOT DIRECT COMMAND".
     Otherwise, if the command is RUN, make the prompt
     character ($33) non-printing.
     Check the operand table to see if a first filename
     is a legal operand for this command.
     If not, go to A0A0.
     Otherwise, clear the filename buffer (call A095).
     Flush to the next non-blank (call A1A4) and copy
     the filename operand to the first filename buffer.
     Skip forward to a comma if one was not found yet.
     If a second filename is legal for this command, use
     the code above to copy it into the second filename
     buffer.
     Check both filenames to see if they are blank.
     If one was required by the command but not given,
     give a syntax error or pass it through to BASIC.
     (As in the case of LOAD with no operands)
     If all is well, go to A0D1 to continue.
A095 A subroutine to blank both filename buffers.
A0A0 Indicate no filename parsed.
     Check operand table to see if a positional operand
     is expected.
     If not, go to A0D1 to continue.
     Otherwise, call A1B9 to convert the numeric operand.
     If omitted, give syntax error.
     If number converted exceeds 16, give "RANGE ERROR"
     If number is supposed to be a slot number, give
     "RANGE ERROR" if it exceeds 7.
     If number is not a slot number, give "RANGE ERROR" if
     it is zero. (MAXFILES 0 is a no-no)
A0D1 Set defaults for the keyword operands (V=0,L=0,B=0)
A0E8 Get the line offset index and flush to the next
     non-blank, skipping any commas found.
     If we are not yet to the end of the line, go to A10C.
     Check to see if any keywords were given which were
     not allowed for this command.
     If not, go to A17A to process the command.
A10C Lookup the keyword found on the command line in the
     table of valid keywords (A941).
     If not in table, give "SYNTAX ERROR" message.
     Get its bit position in the keywords-given flag.
     If the keyword does not have an operand value, go to
     A164.
     Otherwise, indicate keyword found in flag.
     Convert the numeric value associated with keyword.
     Give "SYNTAX ERROR" message if invalid.
     Check to see if the number is within the acceptable
     range as given in the keyword valid range table at
     A955.
```

Save the value of the keyword in the keyword values table starting at AA66.
Go parse the next keyword. go to A0E8.

A164 Indicate C, I, or O keywords were parsed.
Update the MON value in the keyword value table appropriately.
Go parse the next keyword. go to A0E8.

A17A-A17F Call A180 to process the command, then exit via echo at 9F83.

A180-A192 Do command.
Reset the video intercept state to zero.
Clear the file manager parameter list.
Using the command index, get the address of the command handling routine from the command handler routine table at 9D1E and go to it.
Command handler will exit to caller of this routine.

A193-A1A3 Get next character on command line and check to see if it is a carriage return or a comma.

A1A4-A1AD Flush command line characters until a non-blank is found.

A1AE-A1B8 Clear the file manager parameter list at B5BB to zeros.

A1B9-A1D5 Convert numeric operand from command line. Call either A1D6 (decimal convert) or A203 (hex convert) depending upon the presence or lack thereof of a dollar sign ($).

A1D6-A202 Decimal convert subroutine.

A203-A228 Hexadecimal convert subroutine.

A229-A22D PR#n command handler.
Load the parsed numeric value and exit via FE95 in the monitor ROM.

A22E-A232 IN#n command handler.
Load the parsed numeric value and exit via FE8B in the monitor ROM.

A233-A23C MON command handler.
Add new MON flags to old in AA5E and exit.

A23D-A250 NOMON command handler.
If C was given, put out a carriage return since this line was echoed but its CR was not.
Turn off the proper bits in AA5E and exit.

A251-A262 MAXFILES command handler.
Turn off any EXEC file which is active.
Close all open files (call A316).
Set the new MAXFILES number at AA57.
Go to A7D4 to rebuild the DOS file buffers and exit.

A263-A270 DELETE command handler.
Load the delete file manager opcode (05).
Call the file manager open driver (A2AA) to perform the delete.
Find the file buffer used to do the delete and free it (call A764).
Exit to caller.

A271-A274 LOCK command handler.
Load the lock file manager opcode (07) and go to A277.

A275-A27C UNLOCK command handler.
Load the unlock file manager opcode (08).
A277 Call the file manager open driver (A2AA) to perform the desired function.
Exit to the caller via close (A2EA).

A27D-A280 VERIFY command handler.
Load the verify file manager opcode (0C) and go to A277 to perform function.

A281-A297 RENAME command handler.
Store address of second file name in file manager parameter list.
Load the rename file manager opcode (09).
Call the file manager driver at A2C8.
Exit via close (A2EA).

A298-A2A2 APPEND command handler.
Call A2A3 to OPEN the file.
Read the file byte by byte until a zero is found.
If append flag is on, add one to record number and turn flag off.
Exit via a call to POSITION.

A2A3-A2A7 OPEN command handler.
Set file type as TEXT.
Go to A3D5 to open file.

A2A8-A2E9 Command handler common file management code.
Set opcode to OPEN.
A2AA If no L value was given on the command, use 0001 and store record length value in file manager parmlist.
A2C8 Close file if already open.
Is there an available file buffer?
If not, issue "NO FILE BUFFERS AVAILABLE" message.
Point $40,$41 at the free file buffer.
Copy filename to file buffer (allocates the buffer) (A743).
Copy buffer pointers to file manager parmlist (A74E).
Finish filling in the file manager parmlist (A71A).
Set operation code in parmlist.
Exit through the file manager driver.

A2EA-A2FB CLOSE command handler.
If no filename was given as part of command, go to A316 to close all files.
Otherwise, find the open file buffer for filename (A764).
If no such file open, exit to caller.
Otherwise, close file and free buffer (A2FC).
Go back through CLOSE command handler to make sure there are not more open buffers for the same file.

A2FC-A315 Close a file and free its file buffer.
Find out if this buffer is EXEC's (A7AF).
If so, turn EXEC flag off.
Release the buffer by storing a $00 on its filename field.
Copy file buffer pointers to the file manager parmlist.
Set file manager opcode to CLOSE.
Exit through the file manager driver routine.

A316-A330 Close all open files.
Point to first file buffer (A792).
Go to A320.
A31B Point to next file buffer on chain (A79A).
If at end of chain, exit to caller.
A320 Is this file buffer EXEC's?
If so, skip it and go to A31B.
Is it not in use (open)?
If so, skip it and go to A31B.
Otherwise, close it and free it (A2FC).
Go to A316 to start all over.

A331-A35C BSAVE command handler.
Insure that the A and L keywords were present on the command.
If not, issue "SYNTAX ERROR" message.
Open and verify a B type file (A3D5).
Write the A keyword value as the first two bytes of the file.
Write the L keyword value as the next two bytes of the file.
Use the A value to exit by writing a range of bytes from memory to the file.

A35D-A38D BLOAD command handler.
Open the file, ignoring its type.
Insure the type is B.
If not, issue "FILE TYPE MISMATCH" message.
Otherwise, open B type file and test file type (A3D5)
Read the A value from the first two bytes of file.
If A keyword was not given, use the value just read.
Read L value as next two bytes in file.
Go to A471 to read range of bytes to memory from file

A38E-A396 BRUN command handler.
Call BLOAD command handler to load file into memory.
Replace DOS intercepts.
Exit DOS by jumping to the A address value to begin execution of the binary program.

A397-A3D4 SAVE command handler.
Get the active BASIC type (AAB6).
If INTEGER, go to A3BC.
If APPLESOFT, test $D6 flag to see if program is protected.
If so, issue "PROGRAM TOO LARGE" message.
Otherwise, open and test for A type file (A3D5).
Compute program length (PGMEND-LOMEM).
Write this two byte length to file.
Exit by writing program image from LOMEM as a range of bytes (A3FF).

A3BC Open and test for I type file (A3D5).
Compute program length (HIMEM-PGMSTART).
Write this two byte length to file.
Exit by writing program image from PGMSTART as a range of bytes (A3FF).

A3D5-A3DF Open and test file type.
Set file type wanted in file manager parmlist.
Call A2A8 to open file.
Go to A7C4 to check file type.

A3E0-A3FE Write a 2 byte value to the open file.
Store value to be written in file manager parmlist.
Set write one byte opcodes.
Call file manager driver.
Call it again to write second byte and exit to caller

A3FF-A40F Read/write a range of bytes.
Set the address of the range in file manager parmlist
Set subcode to read or write a range of bytes.
Call the file manager driver.
Close the file.
Exit through the VERIFY command handler to insure data was written ok.

A410-A412 Issue "FILE TYPE MISMATCH" message.

A413-A479 LOAD command handler.
Close all files (A316).
Open the file in question.
Is it an A or I type file?
If not, issue "FILE TYPE MISMATCH" message.
Which BASIC is active?
If INTEGER, go to A450.
Select APPLESOFT BASIC (A4B1). This call could result in DOS losing control if the RAM version must be run.
Read first two bytes of file as length of program.
Add length to LOMEM (program start) to compute program end.
Is program end beyond HIMEM?
If so, close file and issue "PROGRAM TOO LARGE".
Set program end and start of variables pointers.
Read program as range of bytes to program start.
Replace DOS intercepts (A851).
Go to BASIC's relocation routine to convert a RAM APPLESOFT program to ROM and vice versa as needed.

A450 Select INTEGER BASIC (A4B1).
Read length of program (first two bytes in file).
Compute program start (HIMEM-LENGTH).
If zero or less than LOMEM, issue "PROGRAM TOO LARGE" message and close file.
Set program start pointers.
Read program into memory as a range of bytes.
Exit to caller.

A47A-A4AA Read two bytes from file (Address or Length).
Set up parmlist to read two bytes to range length field (AA60).
Call file manager driver.
Store value read as range length in file manager parmlist just in case it was a length.

A4AB-A4B0 Close file and issue "PROGRAM TOO LARGE" message.

A4B1-A4D0 Select desired BASIC.
If desired BASIC is already active, exit to caller.
Save current command index in case we must RUN APPLESOFT.
If INTEGER, go to A59E to select it.
Otherwise, copy primary file name to secondary buffer to save it in case RAM APPLESOFT is needed.
Go to A57A to set APPLESOFT.

A4D1-A4E4 RUN command handler.
If APPLESOFT is active, set RUN intercepted flag so that RUN can complete after APPLESOFT is loaded.
Call LOAD command handler to load the program.
Skip a line on the screen.
Put DOS intercepts back.
Go to the RUN entry point in the current BASIC.

A4E5-A4EF INTEGER BASIC RUN entry point intercept.
Delete all variables (CLR equivalent).
Go to the CHAIN entry point in INTEGER BASIC.

A4F0-A4FB CHAIN command handler.
Call the LOAD command handler to load the program.
Skip a line.
Replace DOS intercepts.
Go to current BASIC's CHAIN entry point.

A4FC-A505 APPLESOFT ROM RUN entry point intercept.
Call APPLESOFT to clear variables.
Reset ONERR.
Go to RUN entry point.

A506-A50D APPLESOFT RAM RUN entry point intercept.
Call APPLESOFT to clear variables.
Reset ONERR.
Go to RUN entry point.

A51C-A51A WRITE command handler.
Call READ/WRITE common code (A526).
Set CSWL state to 5 (WRITE mode line start).
Exit DOS (9F83).

A51B-A525 READ command handler.
Call READ/WRITE common code (A526).
Set READ mode flag in status flags (AA51).
Exit DOS (9F83).

A526-A54E READ/WRITE common code.
Locate the open file buffer for this file (A764).
If not open, open it.
Copy file buffer addresses to file manager parmlist.
If R or B were given on command, copy to parmlist and issue a POSITION call to file manager.
Exit to caller.

A54F-A56D INIT command handler.
If V was given, use it. Otherwise, use 254.
Store first page number of DOS in file manager parmlist.
Call file manager driver to INIT diskette.
Exit through SAVE to store greeting program on disk.

A56E-A579 CATALOG command handler.
Call file manager with CATALOG opcode.
Set new V value as default for future commands.
Exit to caller.

A57A-A59D FP command handler.
Set ROM card, if any, for APPLESOFT (A5B2).
If successful, coldstart DOS (9D84).
Otherwise, set status flag to indicate INTEGER BASIC is active.
Set primary filename buffer to "APPLESOFT".
Set flags to indicate RAM APPLESOFT and coldstart.
Go to RUN command handler.

A59E-A5B1 INT command handler.
Set ROM card, if any, for INTEGER BASIC (A5B2).
If not successful, issue "LANGUAGE NOT AVAILABLE".
Otherwise, clear RUN intercepted flag.
Coldstart DOS (9D84).

A5B2-A5C5 Set ROM to desired BASIC.
(This routine is passed a $4C for APPLESOFT or a $20 for INTEGER, since these bytes appear at $E000 in these BASICs. It will work regardless of which BASIC is onboard)
If desired BASIC is already available, exit.
Try selecting ROM card.
If desired BASIC is now available, exit.
Try selecting onboard ROM.
If desired BASIC is now available, exit.
Otherwise, exit with error return code.

A5C6-A5DC EXEC command handler.
Open the file (A2A3).
Copy file buffer address to EXEC's buffer pointer at AAB4,AAB5.
Set EXEC active flag (AAB3).
Jump into POSITION command handler to skip R lines.

```
A5DD-A60D POSITION command handler.
          Locate the open file buffer (A764).
          If not found, open one as a TEXT file.
          Copy buffer pointers to file manager parmlist.
          If R was not given on command, exit.
     A5F2 Otherwise, test R value for zero and exit if so.
          Decrement R value by one.
          Read file byte by byte until a carriage return (end
          of line - $8D) is reached.
          If at end of file, issue "END OF FILE" message.
          Otherwise, go to A5F2 to skip next record.

A60E-A625 Write one data byte to file.
          Insure that BASIC is running a program (A65E).
          If not, close file and warmstart DOS.
          Set up file manager parmlist to write the data byte
          to the open file.
          Call file manager and exit.

A626-A65B Read one data byte from file.
          Insure that BASIC is running a program (A65E).
          If not, close file and warmstart DOS.
          Set CSWL intercept state to 6 (skip prompt character)
     A630 Read next file byte (A68C).
          If not at end of file, go to A644.
          Otherwise, close file.
          If state is not 3 (EXEC) issue "END OF DATA" message.
          Exit to caller.
     A644 If data byte is lower case character, turn its most
          significant bit off to fool GETIN routine in monitor.
          Store data byte in A register saved at entry to DOS.
          Using line index, turn high bit back on in previous
          data byte stored at $200 (input line buffer) to make
          it lower case if necessary.
          Exit DOS (9FB3).

A65E-A678 Test to see if BASIC is running a program or is in
          immediate command mode.
          If active BASIC is INTEGER, go to A672.
          If line number is greater than 65280 and prompt is
          "]" then APPLESOFT is in immediate mode.
          Otherwise, it is executing a program.
          Exit to caller with appropriate return code.
     A672 Check $D9 to determine whether BASIC is executing a
          program and exit with proper return code.

A679-A681 Close current file and warmstart DOS.

A682-A68B EXEC read one byte from file.
          Select EXEC file buffer.
          Copy file buffer addresses to file manager parmlist.
          Set state to 3 (input echo).
          Go to A62D to read a file byte.

A68C-A69C Read next text file byte.
          Set up file manager parmlist to read one byte.
          Call file manager driver.
          Return to caller with the data byte.
```

```
A69D-A6A7 Set $40,$41 to point to EXEC file buffer.

A6A8-A6C3 File manager driver routine.
          Call the file manager itself (AB06).
          If no errors, exit to caller.
          Otherwise, point $40,$41 at file buffer.
          If found, release it by storing a zero on the file
          name field.
          If error was not "END OF DATA", print error message.
          Otherwise, pretend a $00 was read and return to
          caller.

A6C4-A6D4 Miscellaneous error messages.
     A6C4 "COMMAND SYNTAX ERROR"
     A6C8 "NO FILE BUFFERS AVAILABLE"
     A6CC "PROGRAM TOO LARGE"
     A6D0 "FILE TYPE MISMATCH"

A6D5-A701 Error handler.
          Set warmstart flag and clear status (BFE6).
          If APPLESOFT ONERR is active, go to A6EF.
          Otherwise, print RETURN BELL RETURN.
          Print text of error message (A702).
          Print another RETURN.
     A6EF Replace DOS intercepts.
          If a BASIC program is in execution, pass error code
          to BASIC's error handler.
          Otherwise, warmstart BASIC.

A702-A719 Print text of error message.
          Using the error number as an index, print the message
          text from the message table (A971) byte by byte.
          Last character has most significant bit on.

A71A-A742 Complete file manager parameter list.
          Copy Volume value to parmlist.
          Copy Drive value to parmlist.
          Copy Slot value to parmlist.
          Copy address of primary filename buffer to parmlist.
          Save file buffer address in $40,$41.
          Return to caller.

A743-A74D Copy primary filename to file buffer filename field.

A74E-A75A Copy current buffer pointers to file manager parmlist
          Copy file manager workarea buffer pointer.
          Copy T/S List sector buffer pointer.
          Copy data sector buffer address.
          Copy next file buffer link address.
          Return to caller.

A75B-A763 Reset state to 0 and set warmstart flag.

A764-A791 Locate an open or free file buffer.
          Assume there are no free file buffers by zeroing $45.
          Point $40,$41 at first buffer on chain.
          Go to A773.
     A76E Point $40,$41 at next buffer on chain.
          If at end of chain, exit with file not open code.
```

A773 Get first byte of filename field.
If zero (file buffer free), save file buffer address at $44,$45 as an available buffer and go to A76E.
Otherwise, see if name in primary filename buffer matches the name in this file buffer.
If not, go to A76E to get next buffer.
If so, return to caller with open file found code.

A792-A799 Point $40,$41 at first file buffer on chain.

A79A-A7A9 Point $40,$41 at next file buffer on chain.

A7AA-A7AE Get first byte of file name in file buffer.

A7AF-A7C3 See if current buffer belongs to EXEC.
Is EXEC active?
If not, exit.
If so, does current buffer address match EXEC's?
Return to caller with appropriate code.

A7C4-A7D3 Check file type.
Does file type of open file match desired file type?
If so, exit.
Otherwise, turn lock bit off and test again.
If ok, exit.
Otherwise, close file and issue "FILE TYPE MISMATCH".

A7D4-A850 Initialize (build) DOS file buffer chain.
Set $40,$41 to point to first buffer.
Set counter to MAXFILES value.
A7E5 Store zero on filename field to mark as free.
Set up link pointers in buffer to point to file manager workarea (45 bytes prior to filename field).
Set up link pointer to T/S List sector buffer (-256 bytes from file manager workarea buffer).
Set up link pointer to data sector buffer 256 bytes before that.
Decrement counter.
If zero, go to A82D to set HIMEM.
Otherwise, set link to next file buffer as 38 bytes prior to data sector buffer.
Go to A7E5 to set up next buffer.
A82D Set link of last buffer to $0000.
If INTEGER BASIC is active, go to A846.
Otherwise, set APPLESOFT's HIMEM and STRING START pointers in zeropage to point just below the last buffer.
Exit to caller.
A846 Set INTEGER BASIC's HIMEM and PROGRAM START pointers to point just below the last buffer.
Exit to caller.

A851-A883 Replace DOS keyboard/video intercept vectors.
Is DOS keyboard (KSWL) vector still set?
If so, go to A86A.
Otherwise, save current KSWL vector ($38,$39) at AA55,AA56 and replace with DOS intercept routine's address.

A86A Is DOS video (CSWL) vector still set?
If so, exit to caller.
Otherwise, save current CSWL vector ($36,$37) at AA53,AA54 and replace with DOS intercept routine's address.
Exit to caller.

A884-A908 DOS command name text table.
This table consists of the ASCII name for each DOS command in order of command index values, with the last character of each indicated by the MSB being on. Commands in order are:
INIT,LOAD,SAVE,RUN,CHAIN,DELETE,LOCK,UNLOCK,CLOSE, READ,EXEC,WRITE,POSITION,OPEN,APPEND,RENAME, CATALOG,MON,NOMON,PR#,IN#,MAXFILES,FP,INT,BSAVE, BLOAD,BRUN,VERIFY.

Example: INIT is $49 $4E $49 $D4 (I N I T)

A909-A940 Command valid keywords table.
This table is used to determine which keywords are required or may be given for any DOS command.
Each command has a two byte entry with 16 flags, indicating which keywords may be given. The flag bit settings are as follows:

BIT	MEANING
0	Filename legal but optional
1	Command has no positional operand
2	Filename #1 expected
3	Filename #2 expected
4	Slot number positional operand expected
5	MAXFILES value expected as positional operand
6	Command may only be issued from within a program
7	Command may create a new file if file not found
8	C, I, O keywords legal
9	V keyword legal
10	D keyword legal
11	S keyword legal
12	L keyword legal
13	R keyword legal
14	B keyword legal
15	A keyword legal

Thus, for a typical command, OPEN, where the value is $2378, bits 2, 6, 7, 9, 10, 11, and 12 are set so the command has one filename operand, may only be issued from within a program, may create a new file, and the V, D, S, and L keywords are legal.

```
The command entries are:
     INIT        2170
     LOAD        A070
     SAVE        A170
     RUN         A070
     CHAIN       2070
     DELETE      2070
     LOCK        2070
     UNLOCK      2070
     CLOSE       6000
     READ        2206
     EXEC        2074
     WRITE       2206
     POSITION    2204
     OPEN        2378
     APPEND      2270
     RENAME      3070
     CATALOG     4070
     MON         4080
     NOMON       4080
     PR#         0800
     IN#         0800
     MAXFILES    0400
     FP          4070
     INT         4000
     BSAVE       2179
     BLOAD       2071
     BRUN        2071
     VERIFY      2070
```

A941-A94A Keyword name table.
This table contains all the ASCII names of the DOS keywords in standard order. Each keyword name occupies one byte:

V,D,S,L,R,B,A,C,I,O

A94B-A954 Keyword flag bit positions table.
This table gives the bit positions for each keyword into the second byte of the command valid keyword table above and in the flag (AA65) which indicates which keywords were present on the command line.
The bit positions are:

```
V - 40
D - 20
S - 10
L - 08
R - 04
B - 02
A - 01
C - C0 ...
I - A0 ... not used in valid keyword table
O - 90 ...
```

A955-A970 Keyword value valid range table.
This table indicates the range any keyword value may legally have. Each keyword has a four byte entry, two bytes of minimum value, and two bytes of maximum value. Values are:

KEYWORD	MIN	MAX
V	0	254
D	1	2
S	1	7
L	1	32767
R	0	32767
B	0	32767
A	0	65535

C, I, and O do not appear in this table since they do not have numeric values.

A971-AA3E Error message text table.
This table contains the text for each error code in order of error code number:

NUMBER	TEXT
0	RETURN BELL RETURN
1	"LANGUAGE NOT AVAILABLE"
2	"RANGE ERROR" (Bad file manager opcode)
3	"RANGE ERROR" (Bad file manager subcode)
4	"WRITE PROTECTED"
5	"END OF DATA"
6	"FILE NOT FOUND"
7	"VOLUME MISMATCH"
8	"I/O ERROR"
9	"DISK FULL"
10	"FILE LOCKED"
11	"SYNTAX ERROR"
12	"NO BUFFERS AVAILABLE"
13	"FILE TYPE MISMATCH"
14	"PROGRAM TOO LARGE"
15	"NOT DIRECT COMMAND"

AA3F-AA4F Error message text offset index table.
This table contains the offset in bytes to the text of any given error message in the table above. Entries are one byte each for each error code number.

AA4F-AA65 DOS main routines variables.

AA4F Current file buffer address (2 bytes).
AA51 Status flags: $01=READ state, $00=Warmstart,
$80=Coldstart, $40=APPLESOFT RAM
AA52 DOS CSWL intercept state number.
AA53 Address of true CSWL handler (2 bytes).
AA55 Address of true KSWL handler (2 bytes).
AA57 MAXFILES value.
AA59 Save area for S, X, Y, and A registers when DOS is entered (4 bytes).
AA5D Command line index value (offset into line).
AA5E MON flags: (C=$40, I=$20, O=$10)
AA5F Index of last command times 2.
AA60 Range length for LOAD and BLOAD (2 bytes).
AA62 Index of pending command, if any.
AA63 Scratch variable (counter, message index, etc.)
AA64 Index of current keyword.
AA65 Keywords present on command line flags.

AA66-AA74 Keyword values parsed from command and defaulted.
    AA66 Volume (2 bytes)
    AA68 Drive (2 bytes)
    AA6A Slot (2 bytes)
    AA6C Length (2 bytes)
    AA6E Record (2 bytes)
    AA70 Byte (2 bytes)
    AA72 Address (2 bytes)
    AA74 MON value (one byte)

AA75-AA92 Primary file name buffer

AA93-AAB0 Secondary (RENAME) file name buffer

AAB1-AAC0 DOS main routines constants and variables.
    AAB1 MAXFILES default ($03).
    AAB2 Control-D ($84).
    AAB3 EXEC file active flag ($00=not active).
    AAB4 EXEC file buffer address (2 bytes).
    AAB6 Active BASIC flag: $00=INTEGER, $40=APPLESOFT ROM,
    $80=APPLESOFT RAM
    AAB7 RUN intercepted flag.
    AAB8 "APPLESOFT" characters in ASCII (9 bytes)

AAC1-AAC8 File manager constants.
    AAC1 Address of RWTS paramter list (B7E8).
    AAC3 Address of VTOC sector buffer (B3BB).
    AAC5 Address of directory sector buffer (B4BB).
    AAC7 Address of last byte of DOS plus one. (C000)

AAC9-AAE4 File manager function routine entry point table.
This table contains a two byte function handler routine address for each of the 14 file manager opcodes in opcode order.

AAE5-AAF0 File manager read subcode handler entry point table.
This table contains a two byte function handler routine address for each of the 6 read subcodes.

AAF1-AAFC File manager write subcode handler entry point table.
This table contains a two byte function handler routine address for each of the 6 write subcodes.

AAFD-AB05 File manager external entry point (from $3D6).
Is X register zero?
If so, allow new files by simulating an INIT command index.
Otherwise, require old file by simulating a LOAD command index.
Fall through to main file manager entry point.

AB06-AB1E File manager main entry.
Save S register at B39B.
Restore file manager workarea from file buffer (AE6A)
Make sure opcode does not exceed 13.
If it does, return with code=2 (invalid opcode).
Use opcode as index into file manager function routine entry point table and go to proper handler via RTS.

AB1F-AB21 Return with return code=2 (bad opcode).

AB22-AB27 OPEN function handler.
Call common open code (AB28).
Exit file manager.

AB28-ABDB Common open routine.
Initialize file manager workarea by resetting variables to their defaults (ABDC).
Set sector length to 256.
Insure record length is non-zero. If zero, use 1.
Store record length in file manager workarea.
Locate or allocate a directory entry for the file (B1C9).
If file already exists, go to ABA6.
Otherwise, save directory index for free entry.
Using last command index and valid keywords table, determine whether current command may create a new file.
If so, go to AB64.
Otherwise, if running "APPLESOFT", set return code to "LANGUAGE NOT AVAILABLE" and exit.
If not running "APPLESOFT" set return code to "FILE NOT FOUND" and exit.

AB64 Set sector count in directory entry to 1 (there will only be a T/S List sector initially).
Allocate a sector for a T/S List (B244).
Store sector number of this sector in directory entry and in first and current T/S List sector number in file manager workarea.
Store track number in both places also.
Move file type desired to directory entry.
Write directory sector back to catalog (B037).
Select T/S List buffer (AF0C).
Zero it (B7D6).
And write it back (AF3A).
Set return code to 6 ("FILE NOT FOUND").

ABA6 Place track/sector of T/S List in directory entry in first T/S List variable in file manager workarea.
Copy file type from directory to parmlist to pass it back to caller and to file manager workarea.
Copy number of sectors in file to workarea.
Save directory offset to entry in workarea.
Set end of data pointer to "infinity".
Set number of data bytes represented by one T/S List sector to 122*256 (30.5K) in workarea.
Go read first T/S List sector (AF5E).

ABDC-AC05 Initialize file manager workarea.
Zero entire 45 bytes of workarea.
Save complemented volume number in workarea.
Save drive number in workarea.
Save slot*16 in workarea.
Set track number to $11 (catalog track).
Return to caller.

AC06-AC39 CLOSE function handler.
Checkpoint data buffer to disk if needed (AF1D).
Checkpoint T/S List buffer if needed (AF34).
Release any sectors which were preallocated but not used (B2C3).
If VTOC does not need to be re-read, exit.
Otherwise, re-read VTOC sector (AFF7).
Flush through directory sectors in the catalog until we reach the one which contains the entry for this file.
Get the index to the entry.
Update the sector count in the entry to reflect the new file's length.
Checkpoint the directory sector back to the disk.
Exit file manager.

AC3A-AC57 RENAME function handler.
Call common code to locate/open the file.
If file is locked, exit with "FILE LOCKED" return code.
Set $42,$43 to point to new name.
Copy new name to directory entry.
Write back directory sector to disk.
Exit file manager.

AC58-AC69 READ function handler.
Insure subcode does not exceed 5. If so, exit with return code=3.
Use subcode as index into READ subcode handler entry point table.
Go to proper handler of subcode.

AC6A-AC6C Return code = 3, subcode bad

AC6D-AC6F "FILE LOCKED" error return

AC70-AC86 WRITE function handler.
If file is locked, exit with "FILE LOCKED" error.
Insure subcode does not exceed 5. If so, exit with return code=3.
Use subcode as index into WRITE subcode handler entry point table.
Go to proper handler of subcode.

AC87-AC89 POSITION AND READ ONE BYTE subcode handler
Call position routine.
Fall through to next subcode handler.

AC8A-AC92 READ ONE BYTE subcode handler.
Read next file byte (ACA8).
Store in parmlist for pass back to caller.
Exit the file manager.

AC93-AC95 POSITION AND READ A RANGE OF BYTES subcode handler.
Call position routine.
Fall through to next subcode handler.

AC96-ACA7 READ A RANGE OF BYTES subcode handler.
Decrement and check length (B1B5).
Read a byte (ACA8).
Point $42,$43 at range address and add one to address
Store byte read at address.
Loop back to AC96. (length check will exit file manager when length is zero.)

ACA8-ACBA Read a data byte.
Read next data sector if necessary (B0B6).
If at end of file, exit with "END OF DATA" error.
Otherwise, load data byte from data sector buffer.
Increment record number/byte offset into file (B15B).
Increment file position offset (B194).
Return with data byte read.

ACBB-ACBD POSITION AND WRITE ONE BYTE subcode handler.
Call position routine.
Fall through to next subcode handler.

ACBE-ACC6 WRITE ONE BYTE subcode handler.
Find data byte to be written.
Write it to file (ACDA).
Exit file manager.

ACC7-ACC9 POSITION AND WRITE A RANGE OF BYTES subcode handler.
Call position routine.
Fall through to next subcode handler.

ACCA-ACD9 WRITE A RANGE OF BYTES subcode handler.
Copy and advance range address pointer.
Get next byte to write.
Write it to file (ACDA).
Test and decrement length (B1B5).
Loop back to ACCA.

ACDA-ACEE Write a data byte.
Read the proper data sector (if necessary) (B0B6).
Store data byte to be written in sector buffer.
Flag data sector buffer as requiring rewrite.
Increment record number/byte offset into file (B15B).
Exit via file position offset increment routine (B194).

ACEF-ACF5 LOCK function handler.
Set mask byte to $80 (lock).
Go to common code (ACFB).

ACF6-ACFA UNLOCK function handler.
Set mask byte to $00 (unlock).
Fall through to common code.

ACFB-AD11 LOCK/UNLOCK common code.
Locate/open file (AB28).
Get index into directory to entry.
Update file type byte to lock ($8X) or unlock ($0X).
Write directory sector back to disk.
Exit file manager.

```
AD12-AD17 POSITION function handler.
          Call position routine.
          Exit file manager.

AD18-AD2A VERIFY function handler.
          Locate/open file (AB28).
     AD1B Read next data sector.
          If at end of file, exit file manager.
          Otherwise, increment sector position.
          And loop back to AD1B.

AD2B-AD88 DELETE function handler.
          Locate/open file (AB28).
          Using directory index, determine if file is locked.
          If so, exit with "FILE LOCKED" error code.
          Copy T/S List sector's track number from directory to
          workarea and to last character of file name in the
          directory entry itself.
          Store a $FF over T/S List sector's track number in
          directory entry to mark file deleted.
          Copy T/S List sector's sector number to workarea.
          Write directory sector back to disk.
     AD54 Read next T/S List sector (AF5E).
          If no more exist, write VTOC and exit file manager.
          Otherwise, select T/S List buffer (AF0C).
          Index to first T/S pair.
     AD5E If track number is zero or minus, skip it.
          Otherwise, free the data sector by updating the VTOC
          bit map (AD89).
          Index to next T/S pair.
          If more, go to AD5E.
          Get T/S of next T/S List sector from this one.
          Free this T/S List sector (AD89).
          Go process next one, if any (go to AD54).
          Otherwise, write VTOC and exit file manager.

AD89-AD97 Free a sector.
          Call B2DD to deallocate sector in VTOC bit map.
          Zero the sector allocation area of the workarea.
          Return to caller.

AD98-AE2E CATALOG function handler.
          Initialize file manager workarea (ABDC).
          Set V value to zero (complimented=$FF).
          Read the VTOC sector (AFF7).
          Set up a counter for 22 lines before waiting for
          the keyboard.
          Skip 2 lines on the screen.
          Print "DISK VOLUME ".
          Convert Volume number and print it (AE42).
          Skip 2 more lines.
     ADCA Read next directory sector.
          If no more exist, exit file manager.
          Set index to first entry.
     ADD1 Get track number.
          If zero, exit file manager.
          If minus, skip entry (deleted file).
          Print "*" if file is locked (check file type byte).
          Use file type as index into file type name table at
          B3A7 and print single character found there.
```

Print a blank.
Convert and print the number of sectors in the file.
Print a blank.
Index to filename.
Print file name.
Skip to next line.
Advance index to next directory entry.
If there are more, go to ADD1.
If not, go to ADCA to read next directory sector.
Exit when finished.

AE2F-AE41 Skip a line on CATALOG printout.
Output a carriage return.
Decrement line counter.
If still nonzero, exit.
Otherwise, wait for keyboard keypush.
Then reset counter to 21 lines.
And return to caller.

AE42-AE69 Convert the number stored at $44 to a three character printable number and print it.

AE6A-AE7D Restore file manager workarea from file buffer.
Select file manager workarea buffer.
Set return code in parmlist to zero initially.
Copy 45 byte saved image of file manager workarea in file buffer to real file manager workarea.
Exit to caller.

AE7E-AE8D Save file manager workarea in file buffer.
Select file manager workarea buffer.
Copy 45 byte workarea to file buffer.
Exit to caller.

AE8E-AF07 INIT function handler.
Initialize the file manager workarea (ABDC).
Call RWTS to format the diskette (B058).
Copy V value to VTOC buffer.
Start track to allocate next value at $11.
And direction of allocation as $01 (forward).
Zero VTOC bit map (all sectors in use).
Skipping the first three tracks and track $11, copy the 4 byte bit mask (B3A0) to each track entry in the VTOC bit map to free the sectors. This leaves the first three tracks and the catalog track marked in use.
Zero the directory sector buffer.
Point to directory sector buffer.
Set track $11 in RWTS parmlist.
Set up link from this directory sector to next (track $11, sector-1).
Call RWTS to write directory sector.
Write each sector on track in this way except for sector zero.
On last sector (sector 1) zero link pointer.
Point RWTS parms at DOS load point (B7C2).
Write DOS image onto tracks 0-2 (B74A).
Exit file manager.

AF08-AF1C Select a buffer by setting $42,$43 to point to it.
AF08 Select file manager workarea buffer in file buffer.
AF0C Select T/S List sector buffer in file buffer.
AF10 Select data sector buffer in file buffer.
Exit to caller when $42,$43 are set.

AF1D-AF33 Checkpoint write data sector buffer to disk.
Test flag to see if buffer was changed since last read/write.
If not, exit to caller.
Otherwise, set up RWTS pointer (AFE4).
Call RWTS to write sector.
Reset flag to indicate data sector no longer in need of a checkpoint.
Exit to caller.

AF34-AF4A Checkpoint write T/S List sector buffer to disk.
Test flag to see if buffer was changed since last read/write.
If not, exit to caller.
Otherwise, set up RWTS pointer (AF4B).
Call RWTS to write sector.
Reset flag to indicate T/S List sector no longer in need of checkpoint.
Exit to caller.

AF4B-AF5D Prepare for RWTS call with a T/S List sector.
Copy address of T/S List buffer to RWTS parmlist.
Get track/sector of sector.
Exit to caller.

AF5E-AFDB Read a T/S List sector to file buffer.
(CARRY flag is set at entry to indicate whether the first T/S List for the file is wanted (C=0) or the next (C=1).
Memorize carry flag entry code.
Checkpoint current T/S List sector if necessary.
Set up for RWTS (AF4B).
Select T/S List buffer (AF0C).
Is first or next wanted?
If first, go to AFB5 to continue.
Otherwise, get link to next T/S List from this one.
If link is non-zero, use it to find next one and go to AFB5.
Otherwise, we are out of T/S Lists for this file.
If we are reading file, exit with error code.
Otherwise, allocate a new sector (B244).
Point old T/S List sector to new one's track/sector.
Write old T/S List sector back to disk.
Zero the buffer to form new T/S List sector.
Compute and store the relative sector number of the first sector listed in this sector at +5,+6 into the buffer.
Set RWTS opcode to write new T/S List sector to disk.
AFB5 Set RWTS opcode to read old T/S List (unless we just allocated it above).
Set track and sector and call RWTS to read old list or write new list.
Compute relative sector number of last sector (plus one) in this list and store in workarea.
Exit to caller with normal return code.

```
AFDC-AFE3 Read a data sector.
          Set up for RWTS (AFE4).
          Set RWTS READ opcode and go to RWTS driver to do it.

AFE4-AFF6 Prepare for RWTS with data sector.
          Copy address of data sector buffer to RWTS parmlist.
          Get its track/sector.
          And exit to caller.

AFF7-B010 Read/write the VTOC buffer.
     AFF7 Read VTOC entry, go to AFFD.
     AFFB Write VTOC entry, fall through.
     AFFD Common code.
          Copy VTOC sector buffer address to RWTS parmlist.
          Get its track number and use sector $00.
          Exit through RWTS driver.

B011-B036 Read a directory sector.
          (If CARRY flag is zero on entry, read first directory
          sector. If CARRY is one, read next)
          Memorize entry code.
          Set buffer pointers (B045).
          First or next?
          If first, get track/sector of directory sector from
          VTOC at offset +1,+2.
          Otherwise, get track/sector from directory sector at
          offset +1,+2. If track is zero, exit with error code
          (end of directory).
          Call RWTS to read sector.
          Exit with normal return code.

B037-B044 Write directory sector.
          Set buffer pointers.
          Find its track/sector in workarea.
          Exit through RWTS to write it.

B045-B051 Prepare for RWTS for directory buffer.
          Copy directory buffer address to RWTS parmlist.
          Exit to caller.

B052-B0B5 Read/Write Track/Sector (RWTS) driver.
          Set track/sector in RWTS parmlist.
     B058 Set command code (read,write,etc.)
          If writing, set flag (B5D5).
          Set volume number expected in parmlist.
          Set slot*16 in parmlist.
          Set drive in parmlist.
          Set sector size in parmlist.
          Set IOB type in parmlist ($01).
          Call RWTS, passing parmlist pointer.
          Copy true volume found to file manager parmlist.
          Reset volume expected field in RWTS parmlist.
          If an error did not occur, exit to caller.
          Otherwise, get return code.
          Translate vol mismatch to RC=7, write protected to
          RC=4 and all other errors to RC=8 (I/O error).
          Exit file manager now.
```

B0B6-B133 Read next data sector (if necessary).
Is the current file position in the current data sector now in memory?
If so, go to B12C.
Otherwise, checkpoint data sector buffer.
Is the current file position prior to or after this T/S List's domain?
If not, go to B0F3.
Otherwise, read each T/S List for the file, starting with the first, until the proper one is found.
If it is never found, exit with error (ran off end of file reading).

B0F3 Data is in this T/S List sector.
Compute the displacement to the proper entry in this T/S List sector.
Select the T/S List buffer.
Get the track of the data sector wanted.
If non-zero, go to B114.
Otherwise, if not writing, exit with error (no data to read there).
If writing, allocate a new sector and store its track/sector location in the list at this point (B134).
Go to B120.

B114 Read old data sector, using the track/sector found in the T/S List entry.

B120 Save number of sector last read in workarea.

B12C Select data buffer.
Get byte offset and exit normally to caller.

B134-B15A Add a new data sector to file.
Allocate a sector (B244).
Put track/sector numbers in T/S List entry.
Select data buffer and zero it.
Set flags to indicate that the T/S List sector and the data sector buffer require checkpoints.
Exit to caller.

B15B-B193 Increment record number and byte offset into file.
Copy current record number and byte offset to file manager parameter list to pass back to caller.
Increment byte offset in workarea.
If byte offset equals record length, set byte offset back to zero and increment record number.
Return to caller.

B194-B1A1 Increment file position offset.
Increment byte offset into current sector by one.
If at end of sector, increment sector number by one.
Return to caller.

B1A2-B1B4 Copy and advance range address.
Copy range address from file manager parmlist to $42.
Increment range address in parmlist for next time through.
Return to caller.

B1B5-B1C8 Decrement range length.
Decrement range length in file manager parmlist by one.
If zero, exit file manager.
Otherwise, exit to caller.

B1C9-B21B Locate or allocate a directory entry in the catalog.
Read the VTOC sector (AFF7).
Set $42,$43 to point to file name we are looking for.
Set pass number to one (locate file).
B1D8 Initialize directory sector offset (first sector).
B1E1 Increment sector offset.
Read directory sector.
If at end of directory, go to B23A.
Set entry index to first file entry.
B1EB Get track.
If deleted, skip entry, go to B217.
If empty, end of directory, go to B212.
Advance index to filename in directory.
Compare against filename wanted.
If they match, return entry index and exit.
B20B If not, advance index to next entry in sector and loop back to B1EB.
If at end of sector, go to B1E1 to get next sector.
B212 If pass number is one, go to B1D8 to start second pass.
B217 If pass number is one, go to B20B to skip entry.
If second pass, fall through to allocate entry.

B21C-B22F Copy file name to directory entry.
Advance index to file name field in directory entry.
Copy 30 byte filename to directory entry.
Reload directory index and return to caller.

B230-B239 Advance index to next directory entry in sector.
Add 35 (length of entry) to index.
Test for end of sector and return to caller.

B23A-B243 Switch to second pass in directory scan.
If on pass one, switch to pass 2 and go to B1D8.
If on pass two, exit file manager with "DISK FULL" error.

B244-B2C2 Allocate a disk sector.
Is there a track currently allocated to this file?
If not, go to B26A to find a track with free sectors.
B249 Otherwise, decrement sector number to get next possible free sector number.
If there are no more sectors on this track, go to B265 to find a new track.
Otherwise, rotate the track bit mask by one position and get the bit for this sector.
If the sector is in use, loop back to B249.
Otherwise, add one to file's sector count.
Pass back sector number (track number is at B5F1).
And return to caller.
B265 Indicate no track is being used at present.
B26A Reset allocation flag to allow at least one complete search of all tracks for some space.
Read VTOC sector.

B272 Get last track allocated from and add direction value to get next track to examine (+1 or -1).
Are we back to track 0?
If so, go to B284.
Otherwise, are we past track 34?
If so, reverse direction and go to B28E.

B284 Is this the second time we have come to track 0 ? (check allocation flag).
If so, exit with "DISK FULL" error.
Otherwise, set allocation flag to remember this.
Set direction to forward (+1).

B28E Begin at directory track (17 + or - 1).
Compute bit map index (tracknumber*4).
Copy track bit map from VTOC to workarea, watching to see if all four bytes are zero (track is full).
In any case, set all four bytes in VTOC to zero (allocate all sectors).
If no free sectors in the track, go to B272 to try next track.
Otherwise, write VTOC to disk to insure file's integrity.
Set sector number to last sector in track.
Go to B249 to allocate one of its free sectors to the file.

B2C3-B2DC Release pre-allocated sectors in current track and checkpoint the VTOC.
Has a track been allocated to the file?
If not, exit to caller.
Otherwise, read VTOC.
Get next sector which could have been used (number of times track map was shifted during allocation).
Call B2DD to shift track bit map back and merge it back into the VTOC bit map.
Indicate no track has been allocated.
Exit to caller.

B2DD-B2FF Free one or more sectors by shifting mask in file manager's allocation area back into VTOC bit map. (If CARRY is set, current sector is freed also)
Rotate entire 4 byte track bit mask once.
Repeat for as many sectors as were allocated.
Compute index into VTOC for this track's map.
If zero, exit.
Merge ("OR") file manager's bits with those already in VTOC, freeing sectors which were never used by the file.
Return to caller.

B300-B35E Calculate file position.
Set record number passed in file manager parmlist in workarea and in sector offsets.
Clear sector offset high part.
Perform a 16 bit multiply as follows:
3 byte file position = record number times record length.
Add the byte offset from the parmlist into the three byte file position value (B5E4,B5E5,B5E6).
Return to caller.

```
B35F-B37D Error exits.
     B35F RC=1 "LANGUAGE NOT AVAILABLE"
     B363 RC=2 "RANGE ERROR" (bad opcode)
     B367 RC=3 "RANGE ERROR" (bad subcode)
     B36B RC=4 "WRITE PROTECTED"
     B36F RC=5 "END OF DATA"
     B373 RC=6 "FILE NOT FOUND"
     B377 RC=9 "DISK FULL" (all files closed)
     B37B RC=A "FILE LOCKED"

B37F-B396 Exit file manager.
     B37F Exit with no errors.
          Get return code of zero.
          Clear carry flag and go to B386.
     B385 Set carry flag to indicate error.
     B386 Save return code in parmlist.
          Clear monitor status register ($48) after RWTS has
          probably tromped on it.
          Save file manager workarea to file buffer (AE7E).
          Restore processor status and stack register.
          Exit to original caller of file manager.

B397-B3A3 File manager scratch space.
     B397 Track/sector of current directory sector (2 bytes).
     B39B S register save area.
     B39C Directory index.
     B39D Catalog line counter/Directory lookup flag/Etc.
     B39E LOCK/UNLOCK mask/Allocation flag/Etc.
     B3A0 Four byte mask used by INIT to free an entire track
          in the VTOC bit map.

B3A4-B3A6 Decimal conversion table (1,10,100).

B3A7-B3AE File type name table used by CATALOG.
          File types are: T,I,A,B,S,R,A,B, corresponding to
          hex values: $00, $01, $02, $04, $08, $10, $20, and
          $40 respectively.

B3AF-B3BA ASCII text "DISK VOLUME " backwards. Used by CATALOG.

B3BB-B4BA VTOC sector buffer.
     B3BC Track/sector of first directory sector.
     B3BE DOS release number (1, 2, or 3).
     B3C1 Volume number of diskette.
     B3E2 Number of entries in each T/S List sector.
     B3EB Track to allocate next.
     B3EC Direction of track allocation (+1 or -1)
     B3EF Number of tracks on a disk.
     B3F0 Number of sectors on a disk.
     B3F1 Sector size in bytes (2 bytes)
     B3F3 Track 0 bit map
     B3F7 Track 1 bit map
          etc.
     B47B Track 34 bit map
```

```
B4BB-B5BA DIRECTORY sector buffer.
     B4BC Track/sector of next directory sector.
     B4C6 First directory entry and
          Track of T/S List
     B4C7 Sector of T/S List
     B4C8 File type and lock bit
     B4C9 Filename field (30 bytes)
     B4E7 Size of file in sectors (including T/S List(s)).

B5BB-B5D0 File manager parameter list.
     B5BB Opcode
     B5BC Subcode
     B5BD Eight bytes of variable parameters depending on
          opcode.
     B5C5 Return code.
     B5C7 Address of file manager workarea buffer.
     B5C9 Address of T/S List sector buffer.
     B5CB Address of data sector buffer.
     B5CD Address of next DOS buffer on chain (not used).

B5D1-B5FD File manager workarea.
     B5D1 1st T/S List sector's track/sector.
     B5D3 Current T/S List sector's track/sector.
     B5D5 Flags: 80=T/S List needs checkpoint
                 40=Data sector needs checkpoint
                 20=VTOC sector needs checkpoint
                 02=Last operation was write
     B5D6 Current data sector's track/sector.
     B5D8 Directory sector index for file entry.
     B5D9 Index into directory sector to directory entry for
          file.
     B5DA Number of sectors described by one T/S List.
     B5DC Relative sector number of first sector in list.
     B5DE Relative sector number +1 of last sector in list.
     B5E0 Relative sector number of last sector read.
     B5E2 Sector length in bytes.
     B5E4 File position (3 bytes) sector offset, byte offset
          into that sector.
     B5E8 Record length from OPEN.
     B5EA Record number.
     B5EC Byte offset into record.
     B5EE Number of sectors in file.
     B5F0 Sector allocation area (6 bytes).
          Next sector to allocate (shift count)
          Track being allocated
          Four byte bit map of track being allocated, rotated
          to next sector to allocate.
     B5F6 File type.
     B5F7 Slot number times 16.
     B5F8 Drive number.
     B5F9 Volume number (complemented).
     B5FA Track number.

B5FE-B5FF Not used.
```

```
B600-B6FF Start of Boot 2/RWTS image.
     B600 Boot 1 image which can be written to INITed disks
          on track 0, sector 0.
     B65D DOS 3.3 patch area.
     B65D APPEND patch flag.
     B65E APPEND patch. Come here when file manager driver
          gets an error other than end of data.
          Locate and free the file buffer.
          Clear the APPEND flag.
          Get the error number and go print error (A6D2).
     B671 APPEND patch. Come here from APPEND command handler
          to increment record number if APPEND flag is set and
          to clear the flag. Exit through POSITION.
     B686 VERIFY patch. Come here from I/O a range of bytes
          routine to exit through VERIFY after SAVE or BSAVE.
     B692 APPEND patch. Come here from file manager driver if
          return code was END OF DATA.
          Test the file position for zero.
          If non-zero, set APPEND flag on and return to caller.
          If zero (at start of file), copy record number and
          byte offset to file manager parmlist and return a
          zero data byte to caller.
     B6FE Page address of first page in Boot 2.
     B6FF Number of sectors (pages) in Boot 2.

B700-B749 DOS 2nd stage boot loader.
          Set RWTS parmlist to read DOS from disk.
          Call Read/Write group of pages ($B793).
          Create new stack.
          Call SETVID ($FE93) and SETKBD ($FE89).
          Exit to DOS coldstart ($9D84).

B74A-B78C Put DOS on tracks 0-2.
          Set RWTS parmlist to write DOS to disk.
          Call Read/Write group of pages ($B793).
          Exit to caller.

B78D-B792 Unused.

B793-B7B4 Read/Write a group of pages.
          call RWTS through external entry point ($B7B5).
          Exit to caller.

B7B5-B7C1 Disable interrupts and call RWTS.

B7C2-B7D5 Set RWTS parameters for writing DOS.

B7D6-B7DE Zero current buffer.
          Zero 256 bytes pointed to by $42,$43.
          Exit to caller.

B7DF-B7E7 DOS 2nd stage boot loader parmlist.
     B7DF Unused.
     B7E0 Number of pages in 2nd DOS load.
     B7E1 Number of sectors to read/write.
     B7E2 Number of pages in 1st DOS load.
     B7E3 INIT DOS page counter.
     B7E4 Pointer to RWTS parmlist (2 bytes).
     B7E6 Pointer to 1st stage boot location (2 bytes).
```

```
B7E8-B7F8 RWTS parmlist.
     B7E8 Table type. Must be $01.
     B7E9 Slot number times 16.
     B7EA Drive number ($01 or $02).
     B7EB Volume number expected (0 matches any volume).
     B7EC Track number ($00 to $22).
     B7ED Sector number ($00 to $0F).
     B7EE Pointer to Device Characteristics Table (2 bytes).
     B7F0 Pointer to user data buffer for READ/WRITE (2 bytes).
     B7F2 Unused.
     B7F3 Byte count for partial sector (use $00 for 256).
     B7F4 Command code: 0=SEEK, 1=READ, 2=WRITE, 4=FORMAT.
     B7F5 Error code:(valid if carry set) $10=Write protect,
          $20=Volume mismatch, $40=Drive error, $08=INIT error.
     B7F6 Volume number found.
     B7F7 Slot number found.
     B7F8 Drive number found.

B7F9-B7FA Unused.

B7FB-B7FE Device Characteristics Table (DCT).
     B7FB Device type (should be $00).
     B7FC Phases per track (should be $01).
     B7FD Motor on time count (2 bytes - should be $EF, $D8).

B7FF      Unused.

B800-B829 PRENIBBLE routine.
          Converts 256 (8 bit) bytes to 342 (6 bit) "nibbles"
          of the form 00XXXXXX.
          Pointer to page to convert stored at $3E,$3F.
          Data stored at primary and secondary buffers.
          On entry: $3E,$3F contain pointer to user data.
          On exit:  A-reg:unknown
                    X-reg:$FF
                    Y-reg:$FF
                    Carry set

          Exit to caller.

B82A-B8B7 WRITE routine.
          Writes prenibbilized data from primary and secondary
          buffers to disk.
          Calls Write a byte subroutine.
          Writes 5 bytes autosync, starting data marks
          ($D5/$AA/$AD), 342 bytes data, one byte checksum, and
          closing data marks ($DE/$AA/$EB).
          Uses Write Translate Table ($BA29).
          On entry: X-reg:Slot number times 16
          On exit:  Carry set if error
                    If no error:
                    A-reg:unknown
                    X-reg:unchanged
                    Y-reg:$00
                    Carry clear
                    Uses $26,$27,$678
          Exit to caller.

B8B8-B8C1 Write a byte subroutine.
          Timing critical code used to write bytes at 32 cycle
          intervals.
          Exit to caller.
```

```
B8C2-B8DB POSTNIBBLE routine.
          Converts 342 (6 bit) "nibbles" of the form 00XXXXXX
          to 256 (8 bit) bytes.
          Nibbles stored at primary and secondary buffers.
          Pointer to data page stored at $3E,$3F.
          On entry: X-reg:Slot number times 16
                    $3E,$3F:pointer to user data
                    $26:byte count in secondary buffer ($00)
          On exit:  A-reg:unknown
                    X-reg:unknown
                    Y-reg:byte count in secondary buffer
                    Carry set
          Exit to caller.

B8DC-B943 READ routine.
          Read a sector of data from disk and store it at
          primary and secondary buffers.  (First uses secondary
          buffer high to low, then primary low to high)
          On entry: X-reg:Slot times 16
                    Read mode (Q6L,Q7L)
          On exit:  Carry set if error.
                    If no error:
                    A-reg:$AA
                    X-reg:unchanged
                    Y-reg:$00
                    Carry clear
                    Uses $26
          Exit to caller.

B944-B99F RDADR routine.
          Read an Address Field.
          Reads starting address marks ($D5/$AA/$96), address
          information (volume/track/sector/checksum), and
          closing address marks ($DE/$AA).
          On entry: X-reg:Slot number times 16
                    Read mode (Q6L,Q7L)
          On exit:  Carry set if error.
                    If no error:
                    A-reg:$AA
                    X-reg:unchanged
                    Y-reg:$00
                    Carry clear
                    $2F: Volume number found
                    $2E: Track number found
                    $2D: Sector number found
                    $2C: Checksum found
                    Uses $26,$27
          Exit to caller.

B9A0-B9FF SEEKABS routine.
          Move disk arm to desired track.
          Calls arm move delay subroutine ($BA00).
          On entry: X-reg:Slot number times 16
                    A-reg:Desired track (halftrack for single
                          phase disk).
                    $478:Current track.
```

```
         On exit:  A-reg:unknown
                   X-reg:unchanged
                   Y-reg:unknown
                   $2A and $478:Final track
                   $27:Prior track (if seek needed)
                   Uses: $26,$27,$2A,$2B
         Exit to caller.

BA00-BA10 Arm move delay subroutine.
         Delays a specified number of 100 Usec intervals.
         On entry: A-reg:number of 100 Usec intervals.
                   $46,$47:Should contain motor on time count
                   ($EF,$D8) from Device Characteristics Table
                   $478:Current track.
         On exit:  A-reg:$00
                   X-reg:$00
                   Y-reg:unchanged
                   Carry set
         Exit to caller.

BA11-BA28 Arm move delay table.
         Contains values of 100 Usec intervals used during
         Phase-on and Phase-off of stepper motor.

BA29-BA68 Write Translate Table.
         Contains 6 bit "nibbles" used to convert 8 bit bytes.
         Values range from $96 to $FF.
         Codes with more than one pair of adjacent zeros or
         with no adjacent ones are excluded.

BA69-BA95 Unused. See note on page 8-41.

BA96-BAFF Read Translate Table.
         Contains 8 bit bytes used to convert 6 bit "nibbles".
         Values range from $96 to $FF.
         Codes with more than one pair of adjacent zeros or
         with no adjacent ones are excluded.

BB00-BBFF Primary Buffer.
BC00-BC55 Secondary Buffer.

BC56-BCC3 Write Address Field during initialization.
         Calls Write double byte subroutine.
         Writes number of autosync bytes contained in Y-reg,
         starting address marks ($D5/$AA/$96), address
         information (volume/track/sector/checksum), closing
         address marks ($DE/$AA/$EB).
         On entry: X-reg:Slot number times 16
                   Y-reg:number of autosync to write
                   $3E: $AA
                   $3F: sector number
                   $41: volume number
                   $44: track number
         On exit:  A-reg:unknown
                   X-reg:unchanged
                   Y-reg:$00
                   Carry set
         Exit to caller.
```

BCC4-BCDE Write double byte subroutine.
Timing critical code that encodes address information into even and odd bits and writes it at 32 cycle intervals.
Exit to caller.

BCDF-BCFF Unused.

BD00-BD18 Main entry to RWTS.
Upon entry, store Y-reg and A-reg at $48,$49 as pointers to the IOB.
Initialize maximum number of recals at 1 and seeks at 4.
Check if the slot number has changed. If not, branch to SAMESLOT at $BD34.

BD19-BD33 Update slot number in IOB and wait for old drive to turn off.

BD34-BD53 SAMESLOT
Enter read mode and read with delays to see if disk is spinning.
Save result of test and turn on motor just in case.

BD54-BD73 Move pointers in IOB to zero page for future use.
Device Characteristics Table pointer at $3C,$3D and data buffer pointer at $3E,$3F.
Set up $47 (motor on time) with $D8 from DCT.
Check if the drive number has changed. If not, branch to $BD74.
If so, change test results to show drive off.

BD74-BD8F Select appropriate drive and save drive being used as high bit of $35. 1=drive 1, 0=drive 2.
Get test results. If drive was on, branch to $BD90.
Wait for capacitor to discharge using MSWAIT subroutine at $BA00.

BD90-BDAA Get destination track and go to it using MYSEEK subroutine at $BE5A.
Check test result again and if drive was on, branch to TRYTRK at $BDAB.
Delay for motor to come up to speed.

BDAB-BDBB TRYTRK
Get command code.
If null, exit through ALLDONE at $BE46, turning drive off and returning to caller.
If =4, branch to FORMDSK at $BE0D.
Otherwise, move low bit into carry (set=read, clear=write) and save value on status reg.
If write operation, data is prenibbilized via a call to PRENIB16 at $B800.

BDBC-BDEC Initialize maximum retries at 48 and read an Address Field via RDADR16 at $B944.
If read was good, branch to RDRIGHT at $BDED.
If bad read, decrement retries, and, if still some left try again. Else, prepare to recalibrate.
Decrement recal count. If no more, then indicate drive error via DRVERR at $BE04.
Otherwise, reinitialize reseeks at 4 and recalibrate arm. Move to desired track and try again.

BDED-BE03 RDRIGHT
Verify on correct track. If so branch to RTTRK at $BE10.
If not, set correct track via SETTRK subroutine at $BE95 and decrement reseek count.
If not zero then reseek track. If zero, then recal.

BE04-BE0A DRVERR
Clean up stack and status reg.
Load A-reg with $40 (drive error)
Goto HNDLERR at $BE48.

BE0B-BE0C Used to branch to ALLDONE at $BE46.

BE0D-BF0F FORMDSK
Jump to DSKFORM at $BEAF.

BE10-BE25 RTTRK
Check volume number found against volume number wanted.
If no volume was specified, then no error.
If specified volume doesn't match, load A-reg with $20 (volume mismatch error) and exit via HNDLERR at $BE48.

BE26-BE45 CRCTVOL
Check to see if sector is correct.
Use ILEAV table at $BFB8 for software sector interleaving.
If wrong sector, try again by branching back to TRYADR at $BDC1.
If sector correct, find out what operation to do.
If write, branch to WRIT at $BE51.
Otherwise, read data via READ16 ($B8DC).
If read is good, then postnibble data via POSTNB16 ($B8C2) and return to caller with no error.

BE46-BE47 ALLDONE
Skip over set carry instruction in HNDLERR.

BE48-BE50 HNDLERR
Set carry.
Store A-reg in IOB as return code.
Turn off motor.
Return to caller.

BE51-BE59 WRITE
Write a sector using WRITE16 ($B82A).
If the write was good, exit via ALLDONE ($BE46).
If bad write, load A-reg with $10 (write protect error) and exit via HNDLERR ($BE48).

BE5A-BE8D MYSEEK
Provides necessary housekeeping before going to SEEKABS routine.
Determines number of phases per track and stores track information in appropriate slot dependent location.

BE8E-BE94 XTOY routine.
Put slot in Y-reg by transferring X-reg divided by 16 into Y-reg.

BE95-BEAE Set track number.

BEAF-BF0C INIT command handler
Provides setup for initializing a disk.
Get the desired volume number from the IOB.
Zero both the primary and secondary buffers.
Recalibrate the disk arm to track 0.
Set the number of sync bytes to be written between sectors to $28 (40.).
Call TRACK WRITE routine for the actual formatting.
Allow 48 retries during initialization.
Double check that the first sector found is zero after calling TRACK WRITE.
Increment the track number after successfully formatting a track.
Loop back until 35 tracks are done.

BF0D-BF61 TRACK WRITE routine.
Start with sector zero.
Preceed it with 128 self-sync bytes.
Follow them with sectors 0 through 15 in sequence.
Set retry count for verifying the track at 48.
Fill the sector initilization map with positive numbers.
Loop through a delay period to bypass most of the initial self-sync bytes.
Read the first Address Field found.
If the read is good and sector zero was found, enter the VERIFY TRACK routine.
Decrement the sync count by 2 (until it reaches 16 at which time it is decremented by 1).
If sync count is greater than or equal to 5, exit via $BF71.
If not, set carry and return to caller.

BF62-BF87 VERIFY TRACK routine.
This routine reads all 16 sectors from the track that was just formatted.
If an error occurs during the read of either the Address Field or the Data Field, the number of retries is decremented.
The routine continues reading until retries is zero.
Calls Sector Map routine ($BF88).

BF88-BFA7 Sector Map routine.
This routine marks the sector initialization map as each sector is verified.
If an error occurs, the routine exits through $BF6C, which decrements the number of retries and continues if that value is greater than zero.
Upon completion of track zero, the sync count is decremented by two if it is at least 16.

BFA8-BFB7 Sector Initialization Map used to mark sectors as they are initialized.
Contains a $30 prior to initialization of a track.
Value changed to $FF as each sector is completed.

BFB8-BFC7 Sector Translate Table
Sector interleaving done with software.

BFC8-BFD8 Patch area starts here.
Patch from $B741 to zero language card during boot.
Call SETVID ($FE93).
Unprotect Language Card (if present).
Store $00 at $E000.
Exit through SETKBD ($FE89) and DOS coldstart.

BFD9-BFDB Unused. See note below.

BFDC-BFE5 Patch called from $A0E2.
Set three additional defaults (Byte offset=0).
Return to caller.

BFE6-BFEC Patch called from $A6D5.
Call $A75B to reset state and set warmstart flag.
Mark RUN not interrupted.
Return to caller.

BFED-BFFF Patch called from $B377.
Call $AE7E to save file manager workarea.
Restore stack.
Close all open files ($A316).
Save stack again.
Exit through $B385 ("DISK FULL ERROR").

NOTE: In January 1983, minor revisions were made to DOS 3.3 (see page 2-4). The area from BA69-BA93, which was previously unused, was used to add three new patches. The second of these patches is an extension of the previous patch at $BFC8, and requires the use of $BFD9-$BFDB, previously unused. The three patches are documented below.

BA69-BA75 Patch called from $A6BB.
Clears the APPEND flag ($B65D) if last command was APPEND. Return to caller.

BA76-BA81 Patch called from $BFD6.
Set MODE flag to $FF (used by Apple 80-column firmware). Turn off 80-column display.
Turn off alternate character set.
Exit through $FB2F (Monitor INIT).

BA84-BA93 Patch called from $B683.
Set file manager parameters, byte offset, and record number to zero. Save stack in stack register save area.
Exit through $B37F (exit file manager).

In addition, the calculate file position routine ($B300-$B35E) has been modified to clear the carry before adding the byte offset to the current byte position.

DOS ZERO PAGE USAGE

BYTE	USE
24	Cursor horizontal (DOS)
26,27	Sector read buffer address (ROM)
	Scratch space (RWTS)
28,29	BASL/BASH (DOS)
2A	Segment merge counter (ROM,BOOT)
	Scratch space (RWTS)
2B	BOOT slot*16 (ROM)
	Scratch space (RWTS)
2C	Checksum from sector header (RWTS)
2D	Sector number from sector header (RWTS)
2E	Track number from sector header (RWTS)
2F	Volume number from sector header (RWTS)
33	Prompt character (DOS)
35	Drive number in high bit (RWTS)
36,37	CSWL,CSWH (DOS)
38,39	KSWL,KSWH (DOS)
3C	Workbyte (ROM)
	Merge workbyte (BOOT)
	Device characteristics table address (RWTS)
3D	Sector number (ROM)
	Device characteristics table address (RWTS)
3E,3F	Address of ROM sector-read subroutine (BOOT)
	Buffer address (RWTS)
40,41	DOS image address (BOOT)
	File buffer address (DOS)
41	Format track counter (RWTS)
42,43	Buffer address (DOS)
44,45	Numeric operand (DOS)
46,47	Scratch space (RWTS)
48,49	IOB address (RWTS)
4A,4B	INTEGER BASIC LOMEM address (DOS)
	Format diskette workspace (RWTS)
4C,4D	INTEGER BASIC HIMEM address (DOS)
67,68	APPLESOFT BASIC PROGRAM START (DOS)
69,6A	APPLESOFT BASIC VARIABLES START (DOS)
6F,70	APPLESOFT BASIC STRING START (DOS)
73,74	APPLESOFT BASIC HIMEM address (DOS)
76	APPLESOFT BASIC line number high (DOS)
AF,B0	APPLESOFT BASIC PROGRAM END (DOS)
CA,CB	INTEGER BASIC PROGRAM START (DOS)
CC,CD	INTEGER BASIC VARIABLES END (DOS)
D6	APPLESOFT BASIC PROGRAM protection flag (DOS)
D8,D9	INTEGER BASIC line number (DOS)
	APPLESOFT BASIC ONERR (DOS)

APPENDIX A
EXAMPLE PROGRAMS

This section is intended to supply the reader with utility programs which can be used to examine and repair diskettes. These programs are provided in their source form to serve as examples of the programming necessary to interface practical programs to DOS. The reader who does not know assembly language may also benefit from these programs by entering them from the monitor in their binary form and saving them to disk for later use. It should be pointed out that the use of 16 sector diskettes is assumed, although most of the programs can be easily modified to work under any version of DOS. It is recommended that, until the reader is completely familiar with the operation of these programs, he would be well advised to use them only on an "expendable" diskette. None of the programs can physically damage a diskette, but they can, if used improperly, destroy the data on a diskette, requiring it to be re-INITialized.

Five programs are provided:

DUMP TRACK DUMP UTILITY

This is an example of how to directly access the disk drive through its I/O select addresses. DUMP may be used to dump any given track in its raw, prenibbilized form, to memory for examination. This can be useful both to understand how disks are formatted and in diagnosing clobbered diskettes.

ZAP DISK UPDATE UTILITY

This program is the backbone of any attempt to patch a diskette directory back together. It is also useful in examining the structure of files stored on disk and in applying patches to files or DOS directly. ZAP allows its user to read, and optionally write, any sector on a diskette. As such, it serves as a good example of a program which calls Read/Write Track/Sector (RWTS).

INIT REFORMAT A SINGLE TRACK

This program will initialize a single track on a diskette. Any volume number ($00-$FF) may be specified. INIT is useful in restoring a track whose sectoring has been damaged without reinitializing the entire diskette. DOS 3.3 and 48K is assumed.

FTS FIND T/S LISTS UTILITY

FTS may be used when the directory for a diskette has been destroyed. It searches every sector on a diskette for what appear to be Track/Sector Lists, printing the track and sector location of each it finds. Knowing the locations of the T/S Lists can help the user patch together a new catalog using ZAP.

COPY CONVERT FILES

COPY is provided as an example of direct use of the DOS File Manager package from assembly language. The program will read an input B-type file and copy its contents to an output T-type file. Although it could be used, for example, to convert files used by the Programma PIE editor for use by the Apple Toolkit assembler, it is not included as a utility program but rather as an example of the programming necessary to access the File Manager.

STORING THE PROGRAMS ON DISKETTE

The enterprising programmer may wish to type the source code for each program into an assembler and assemble the programs onto disk. The Apple Toolkit assembler was used to produce the listings presented here, and interested programmers should consult the documentation for that assembler for more information on the pseudo-opcodes used. For the non-assembly language programmer, the binary object code of each program may be entered from the monitor using the following procedure.

The assembly language listings consist of columns of information as follows:

The address of some object code
The object code which should be stored there
The statement number
The statement itself

For example...

```
0800:20 DC 03  112 COPY    JSR  LOCFPL      FIND PARMLIST
```

indicates that the binary code "20DC03" should be stored at 0800 and that this is statement 112. To enter a program in the monitor, the reader must type in each address and its corresponding object code. The following is an example of how to enter the DUMP program:

```
CALL -151                (Enter the monitor from BASIC)
0800:20 E3 03
0803:84 00
0805:85 01
0807:A5 02

 ...etc...

0879:85 3F
087B:4C B3 FD
BSAVE DUMP,A$800,L$7E    (Save program to disk)
```

Note that if a line (such as line 4 in DUMP) has no object bytes associated with it, it may be ignored. When the program is to be run...

```
BLOAD DUMP               (Load program)
CALL -151                (Get into monitor)
02:11 N 800G             (Store track to dump, run program)
```

The BSAVE commands which must be used with the other programs are:

```
BSAVE ZAP,A$900,L$6C
BSAVE INIT,A$800,L$89
BSAVE FTS,A$900,L$DC
BSAVE COPY,A$800,L$1EC
```

A diskette containing these five programs is available for $9.95 plus shipping charges directly from Quality Software (21601 Marilla Street, Chatsworth, CA 91311).

Also available from Quality Software is an expanded version of these utilities called BAG OF TRICKS. You can find information and an order form on the last page of this book.

DUMP — TRACK DUMP UTILITY

The DUMP program will dump any track on a diskette in its raw, pre-nibbilized format, allowing the user to examine the sector address and data fields and the formatting of the track. This allows the curious reader to examine his own diskettes to better understand the concepts presented in the preceeding chapters. DUMP may also be used to examine most protected disks to see how they differ from normal ones and to diagnose diskettes with clobbered sector address or data fields with the intention of recovering from disk I/O errors. The DUMP program serves as an example of direct use of the DISK II hardware from assembly language, with little or no use of DOS.

To use DUMP, first store the number of the track you wish dumped at location $02, then begin execution at $800. DUMP will return to the monitor after displaying the first part of the track in hexadecimal on the screen. The entire track image is stored, starting at $1000. For example:

```
CALL -151                (Get into the monitor from BASIC)
BLOAD DUMP               (Load the DUMP program)
 ...Now insert the diskette to be dumped...
02:11 N 800G             (Store a 11 (track 17, the catalog
                          track) in $02, N terminates the store
                          command, go to location $800)
```

The output might look like this...

```
1000- D5 AA 96 AA AB AA BB AB   (Start of sector address)
1008- AA AB BA DE AA E8 C0 FF
1010- 9E FF FF FF FF FF D5 AA   (Start of sector data)
1018- AD AE B2 9D AC AE 96 96   (Sector data)
 ...etc...
```

Quite often, a sector with an I/O error will have only one bit which is in error, either in the address or data header or in the actual data itself. A particularly patient programmer can, using DUMP and perhaps a half hour of hand "nibbilizing" determine the location of the error and record the data on paper for later entry via ZAP. A thorough understanding of Chapter 3 is necessary to accomplish this feat.

```
0800:                     ORG  $800

0800:            ************************************************************
0800:            *                                                          *
0800:            * DUMP:THIS PROGRAM WILL ALLOW ITS USER TO DUMP AN ENTIRE *
0800:            *        TRACK IN ITS RAW FORM INTO MEMORY FOR EXAMINATION. *
0800:            *                                                          *
0800:            * INPUT: $02 = TRACK TO BE READ                            *
0800:            *                                                          *
0800:            * OUTPUT:$1000 = ADDRESS OF TRACK IMAGE                    *
0800:            *                                                          *
0800:            * ENTRY POINT: $800                                        *
0800:            *                                                          *
0800:            * PROGRAMMER: DON D WORTH 2/19/81                          *
0800:            *                                                          *
0800:            ************************************************************

0800:            *        ZPAGE DEFINITIONS

0000:            PTR      EQU  $0         WORK POINTER
0002:            TRACK    EQU  $2         TRACK TO BE READ/WRITTEN
003C:            A1L      EQU  $3C        MONITOR POINTER
003E:            A2L      EQU  $3E        MONITOR POINTER
0048:            PREG     EQU  $48        MONITOR STATUS REGISTER

0800:            *        OTHER ADDRESSES

1000:            BUFFER   EQU  $1000      TRACK IMAGE AREA
03E3:            LOCRPL   EQU  $3E3       LOCATE RWTS PARMLIST SUBRTN
03D9:            RWTS     EQU  $3D9       RWTS SUBROUTINE
FDED:            COUT     EQU  $FDED      PRINT ONE CHAR SUBROUTINE
FDB3:            XAM      EQU  $FDB3      MONITOR HEX DUMP SUBRTN

0800:            *        DISK I/O SELECTS

C080:            DRVSM0   EQU  $C080      STEP MOTOR POSITIONS
C081:            DRVSM1   EQU  $C081
C082:            DRVSM2   EQU  $C082
C083:            DRVSM3   EQU  $C083
C084:            DRVSM4   EQU  $C084
C085:            DRVSM5   EQU  $C085
C086:            DRVSM6   EQU  $C086
C087:            DRVSM7   EQU  $C087
C088:            DRVOFF   EQU  $C088      TURN DRIVE OFF AFTER 6 REVS
C089:            DRVON    EQU  $C089      TURN DRIVE ON
C08A:            DRVSL1   EQU  $C08A      SELECT DRIVE 1
C08B:            DRVSL2   EQU  $C08B      SELECT DRIVE 2
C08C:            DRVRD    EQU  $C08C      READ DATA LATCH
C08D:            DRVWR    EQU  $C08D      WRITE DATA LATCH
C08E:            DRVRDM   EQU  $C08E      SET READ MODE
C08F:            DRVWRM   EQU  $C08F      SET WRITE MODE

0800:            *        RWTS PARMLIST DEFINITION

0000:                     DSECT
0000:            RPLIOB   DS   1          IOB TYPE ($01)
0001:            RPLSLT   DS   1          SLOT*16
0002:            RPLDRV   DS   1          DRIVE
0003:            RPLVOL   DS   1          VOLUME
0004:            RPLTRK   DS   1          TRACK
0005:            RPLSEC   DS   1          SECTOR
0006:            RPLDCT   DS   2          ADDRESS OF DCT
0008:            RPLBUF   DS   2          ADDRESS OF BUFFER
000A:            RPLSIZ   DS   2          SECTOR SIZE
000C:            RPLCMD   DS   1          COMMAND CODE
0000:            RPLCNL   EQU  $00           NULL COMMAND
0001:            RPLCRD   EQU  $01           READ COMMAND
0002:            RPLCWR   EQU  $02           WRITE COMMAND
0004:            RPLCFM   EQU  $04           FORMAT COMMAND
000D:            RPLRCD   DS   1          RETURN CODE
0010:            RPLRWP   EQU  $10           WRITE PROTECTED
0020:            RPLRVM   EQU  $20           VOLUME MISMATCH
0040:            RPLRDE   EQU  $40           DRIVE ERROR
0080:            RPLRRE   EQU  $80           READ ERROR
```

```
000E:              RPLTVL  DS   1          TRUE VOLUME
000F:              RPLPSL  DS   1          PREVIOUS SLOT
0010:              RPLPDR  DS   1          PREVIOUS DRIVE
0800:                      DEND

0800:              *       USE RWTS TO POSITION THE ARM TO THE DESIRED TRACK

0800:20 E3 03      DUMP    JSR  LOCRPL     LOCATE RWTS PARMLIST
0803:84 00                 STY  PTR        AND SAVE POINTER
0805:85 01                 STA  PTR+1

0807:A5 02                 LDA  TRACK      GET TRACK TO READ/WRITE
0809:A0 04                 LDY  #RPLTRK    STORE IN RWTS LIST
080B:91 00                 STA  (PTR),Y

080D:A9 00                 LDA  #RPLCNL    NULL OPERATION
080F:A0 0C                 LDY  #RPLCMD    AND STORE IN LIST
0811:91 00                 STA  (PTR),Y

0813:A9 00                 LDA  #0         ANY VOLUME WILL DO
0815:A0 03                 LDY  #RPLVOL
0817:91 00                 STA  (PTR),Y
0819:20 E3 03              JSR  LOCRPL     RELOAD POINTER TO PARMS
081C:20 D9 03              JSR  RWTS       CALL RWTS
081F:A9 00                 LDA  #0
0821:85 48                 STA  PREG       FIX P REG SO DOS IS HAPPY

0823:              *       PREPARE TO DUMP TRACK TO MEMORY

0823:A0 01                 LDY  #RPLSLT    GET SLOT*16
0825:B1 00                 LDA  (PTR),Y
0827:AA                    TAX
0828:BD 89 C0              LDA  DRVON,X    KEEP DRIVE ON
082B:BD 8E C0              LDA  DRVRDM,X   INSURE READ MODE

082E:A9 00                 LDA  #>BUFFER   POINT AT DATA
0830:85 00                 STA  PTR
0832:A9 10                 LDA  #<BUFFER
0834:85 01                 STA  PTR+1
0836:A0 00                 LDY  #0

0838:              *       START DUMPING AT THE BEGINNING OF A SECTOR ADDRESS
0838:              *       FIELD OR A SECTOR DATA FIELD

0838:BD 8C C0      LOOP1   LDA  DRVRD,X    WAIT FOR NEXT BYTE
083B:10 FB                 BPL  LOOP1
083D:C9 FF                 CMP  #$FF       AUTOSYNC?
083F:D0 F7                 BNE  LOOP1      NO, DON'T START IN MIDDLE
0841:BD 8C C0      LOOP2   LDA  DRVRD,X    WAIT FOR NEXT BYTE
0844:10 FB                 BPL  LOOP2
0846:C9 FF                 CMP  #$FF       TWO AUTOSYNCS?
0848:D0 EE                 BNE  LOOP1      NOT YET
084A:BD 8C C0      LOOP3   LDA  DRVRD,X
084D:10 FB                 BPL  LOOP3
084F:C9 FF                 CMP  #$FF       STILL AUTOSYNCS?
0851:F0 F7                 BEQ  LOOP3      YES, WAIT FOR DATA BYTE
0853:D0 05                 BNE  LOOP4      ELSE, START STORING DATA

0855:              *       ONCE ALIGNED, BEGIN COPYING THE TRACK TO MEMORY.
0855:              *       COPY AT LEAST TWICE ITS LENGTH TO INSURE WE GET IT
0855:              *       ALL.

0855:BD 8C C0      LOOPD   LDA  DRVRD,X    WAIT FOR NEXT DATA BYTE
0858:10 FB                 BPL  LOOPD
085A:91 00         LOOP4   STA  (PTR),Y    STORE IN MEMORY
085C:E6 00                 INC  PTR        BUMP POINTER
085E:D0 F5                 BNE  LOOPD
0860:E6 01                 INC  PTR+1
0862:A5 01                 LDA  PTR+1
0864:C9 40                 CMP  #$40       DONE AT LEAST A TRACK?
0866:90 ED                 BCC  LOOPD      NO, CONTINUE
0868:BD 88 C0              LDA  DRVOFF,X   TURN DRIVE OFF
```

```
086B:                *       WHEN FINISHED, DUMP SOME OF TRACK IN HEX ON SCREEN

086B:A9 00           EXIT    LDA  #>BUFFER   DUMP 800.8AF
086D:85 3C                   STA  A1L
086F:A9 10                   LDA  #<BUFFER
0871:85 3D                   STA  A1L+1
0873:A9 AF                   LDA  #>BUFFER+$AF
0875:85 3E                   STA  A2L
0877:A9 10                   LDA  #<BUFFER+$AF
0879:85 3F                   STA  A2L+1
087B:4C B3 FD                JMP  XAM        EXIT VIA HEX DISPLAY

*** SUCCESSFUL ASSEMBLY: NO ERRORS
```

ZAP — DISK UPDATE UTILITY

The next step up the ladder from DUMP is to access data on the diskette at the sector level. The ZAP program allows its user to specify a track and sector to be read into memory. The programmer can then make changes in the image of the sector in memory and subsequently use ZAP to write the modified image back over the sector on disk. ZAP is particularly useful when it is necessary to patch up a damaged directory. Its use in this regard will be covered in more detail when FTS is explained.

To use ZAP, store the number of the track and sector you wish to access in $02 and $03 respectively. Tracks may range from $00 to $22 and sectors from $00 to $0F. For example, the Volume Table of Contents (VTOC) for the diskette may be examined by entering $11 for the track and $00 for the sector. $04 should be initialized with either a $01 to indicate that the sector is to be read into memory, or $02 to ask that memory be written out to the sector. Other values for location $04 can produce damaging results ($04 in location $04 will INIT your diskette!). When these three memory locations have been set up, begin execution at $900. ZAP will read or write the sector into or from the 256 bytes starting at $800. For example:

```
CALL -151                (Get into the monitor from BASIC)
BLOAD ZAP                (Load the ZAP program)
 ...Now insert the diskette to be zapped...
02:11 00 01 N 900G       (Store a 11 (track 17, the catalog
                          track) in $02, a 00 (sector 0) at $03,
                          and a 01 (read) at $04.  N ends the
                          store command and 900G runs ZAP.)
```

The output might look like this...

```
0800- 04 11 0F 03 00 00 01 00   (Start of VTOC)
0808- 00 00 00 00 00 00 00 00
0810- 00 00 00 00 00 00 00 00
0818- 00 00 00 00 00 00 00 00
 ...etc...
```

In the above example, if the byte at offset 3 (the version of DOS which INITed this diskette) is to be changed, the following would be entered...

```
803:02                   (Change 03 to 02)
04:02 N 900G             (Change ZAP to write mode and do it)
```

Note that ZAP will remember the previous values in $02, $03, and $04.

If something is wrong with the sector to be read (an I/O error, perhaps), ZAP will print an error message of the form:

RC=10

A return code of 10, in this case, means that the diskette was write protected and a write operation was attempted. Other error codes are 20 - volume mismatch, 40 - drive error, and 80 - read error. Refer to the documentation on RWTS given in Chapter 6 for more information on these errors.

```
0900:             ORG  $900

0900:        ***********************************************************
0900:        *                                                         *
0900:        * ZAP: THIS PROGRAM WILL ALLOW ITS USER TO READ/WRITE     *
0900:        *      INDIVIDUAL SECTORS FROM/TO THE DISKETTE            *
0900:        *                                                         *
0900:        * INPUT: $02 = TRACK TO BE READ                           *
0900:        *        $03 = SECTOR TO BE READ/WRITTEN                  *
0900:        *        $04 = $01 - READ SECTOR                          *
0900:        *              $02 - WRITE SECTOR                         *
0900:        *        $800 = ADDRESS OF SECTOR DATA BUFFER             *
0900:        *                                                         *
0900:        * ENTRY POINT: $900                                       *
0900:        *                                                         *
0900:        * PROGRAMMER: DON D WORTH 2/15/81                         *
0900:        *                                                         *
0900:        ***********************************************************


0087:        BELL     EQU  $87       BELL CHARACTER

0900:        *        ZPAGE DEFINITIONS

0000:        PTR      EQU  $0        WORK POINTER
0002:        TRACK    EQU  $2        TRACK TO BE READ/WRITTEN
0003:        SECTOR   EQU  $3        SECTOR TO BE READ/WRITTEN
0004:        OPER     EQU  $4        OPERATION TO BE PERFORMED
0001:        READ     EQU  1            READ OPERATION
0002:        WRITE    EQU  2            WRITE OPERATION
003C:        A1L      EQU  $3C       MONITOR POINTER
003E:        A2L      EQU  $3E       MONITOR POINTER
0048:        PREG     EQU  $48       MONITOR STATUS REGISTER

0900:        *        OTHER ADDRESSES

0800:        BUFFER   EQU  $800      SECTOR DATA BUFFER
03E3:        LOCRPL   EQU  $3E3      LOCATE RWTS PARMLIST SUBRTN
03D9:        RWTS     EQU  $3D9      RWTS SUBROUTINE
FDED:        COUT     EQU  $FDED     PRINT ONE CHAR SUBROUTINE
FDDA:        PRBYTE   EQU  $FDDA     PRINT ONE HEX BYTE SUBRTN
FDB3:        XAM      EQU  $FDB3     MONITOR HEX DUMP SUBRTN

0900:        *        RWTS PARMLIST DEFINITION

0000:                 DSECT
0000:        RPLIOB   DS   1         IOB TYPE ($01)
0001:        RPLSLT   DS   1         SLOT*16
0002:        RPLDRV   DS   1         DRIVE
0003:        RPLVOL   DS   1         VOLUME
0004:        RPLTRK   DS   1         TRACK
0005:        RPLSEC   DS   1         SECTOR
0006:        RPLDCT   DS   2         ADDRESS OF DCT
0008:        RPLBUF   DS   2         ADDRESS OF BUFFER
000A:        RPLSIZ   DS   2         SECTOR SIZE
000C:        RPLCMD   DS   1         COMMAND CODE
0000:        RPLCNL   EQU  $00          NULL COMMAND
```

```
0001:                 RPLCRD  EQU  $01          READ COMMAND
0002:                 RPLCWR  EQU  $02          WRITE COMMAND
0004:                 RPLCFM  EQU  $04          FORMAT COMMAND
000D:                 RPLRCD  DS   1         RETURN CODE
0010:                 RPLRWP  EQU  $10          WRITE PROTECTED
0020:                 RPLRVM  EQU  $20          VOLUME MISMATCH
0040:                 RPLRDE  EQU  $40          DRIVE ERROR
0080:                 RPLRRE  EQU  $80          READ ERROR
000E:                 RPLTVL  DS   1         TRUE VOLUME
000F:                 RPLPSL  DS   1         PREVIOUS SLOT
0010:                 RPLPDR  DS   1         PREVIOUS DRIVE
0900:                         DEND


0900:                 *       FILL IN RWTS LIST

0900:20 E3 03         ZAP     JSR  LOCRPL    LOCATE RWTS PARMLIST
0903:84 00                    STY  PTR       AND SAVE POINTER
0905:85 01                    STA  PTR+1

0907:A5 02                    LDA  TRACK     GET TRACK TO READ/WRITE
0909:A0 04                    LDY  #RPLTRK   STORE IN RWTS LIST
090B:91 00                    STA  (PTR),Y

090D:A5 03                    LDA  SECTOR    GET SECTOR TO READ/WRITE
090F:C9 10                    CMP  #16       BIGGER THAN 16 SECTORS?
0911:90 04                    BCC  SOK       NO
0913:A9 00                    LDA  #0
0915:85 03                    STA  SECTOR    YES, PUT IT BACK TO ZERO
0917:A0 05            SOK     LDY  #RPLSEC
0919:91 00                    STA  (PTR),Y   STORE IN RWTS LIST

091B:A0 08                    LDY  #RPLBUF
091D:A9 00                    LDA  #>BUFFER  STORE BUFFER PTR IN LIST
091F:91 00                    STA  (PTR),Y
0921:C8                       INY
0922:A9 08                    LDA  #<BUFFER
0924:91 00                    STA  (PTR),Y

0926:A5 04                    LDA  OPER      GET COMMAND CODE
0928:A0 0C                    LDY  #RPLCMD   AND STORE IN LIST
092A:91 00                    STA  (PTR),Y

092C:A9 00                    LDA  #0        ANY VOLUME WILL DO
092E:A0 03                    LDY  #RPLVOL
0930:91 00                    STA  (PTR),Y

0932:                 *       NOW CALL RWTS TO READ/WRITE THE SECTOR

0932:20 E3 03                 JSR  LOCRPL    RELOAD POINTER TO PARMS
0935:20 D9 03                 JSR  RWTS      CALL RWTS
0938:A9 00                    LDA  #0
093A:85 48                    STA  PREG      FIX P REG SO DOS IS HAPPY
093C:90 1B                    BCC  EXIT      ALL IS WELL

093E:                 *       ERROR OCCURED, PRINT "RC=XX"

093E:A9 87                    LDA  #BELL     BEEP THE SPEAKER
0940:20 ED FD                 JSR  COUT
0943:A9 D2                    LDA  #'R       PRINT THE "RC="
0945:20 ED FD                 JSR  COUT
0948:A9 C3                    LDA  #'C
094A:20 ED FD                 JSR  COUT
094D:A9 BD                    LDA  #'=
094F:20 ED FD                 JSR  COUT
0952:A0 0D                    LDY  #RPLRCD
0954:B1 00                    LDA  (PTR),Y   GET RWTS RETURN CODE
0956:20 DA FD                 JSR  PRBYTE    PRINT RETURN CODE IN HEX
```

```
0959:              *       WHEN FINISHED, DUMP SOME OF SECTOR IN HEX

0959:A9 00         EXIT    LDA  #>BUFFER   DUMP 800.8B7
095B:85 3C                 STA  A1L
095D:A9 08                 LDA  #<BUFFER
095F:85 3D                 STA  A1L+1
0961:A9 AF                 LDA  #>BUFFER+$AF
0963:85 3E                 STA  A2L
0965:A9 08                 LDA  #<BUFFER+$AF
0967:85 3F                 STA  A2L+1
0969:4C B3 FD              JMP  XAM        EXIT VIA HEX DISPLAY

*** SUCCESSFUL ASSEMBLY: NO ERRORS
```

INIT — REFORMAT A SINGLE TRACK

Occasionally the sectoring information on a diskette can become damaged so that one or more sectors can no longer be found by DOS. To correct this problem requires that the sector address and data fields be re-formatted for the entire track thus affected. INIT can be used to selectively reformat a single track, thus avoiding a total re-INIT of the diskette. Before using INIT, the user should first attempt to write on the suspect sector (using ZAP). If RWTS refuses to write to the sector (RC=40), then INIT must be run on the entire track. To avoid losing data, all other sectors on the track should be read and copied to another diskette prior to reformatting. After INIT is run they can be copied back to the repaired diskette and data can be written to the previously damaged sector.

To run INIT, first store the number of the track you wish reformatted at location $02, the volume number of the disk at location $03 (the volume number should match the volume number of the other tracks), and then begin execution at $800. INIT will return to the monitor upon completion. If the track can not be formatted for some reason (eg. physical damage or problems with the disk drive itself) a return code is printed. For example:

```
CALL -151                  (Get into the monitor from BASIC)
BLOAD INIT                 (Load the INIT program)
 ...Now insert the disk to be INIT-ed...
02:11 FE N 800G            (Store a 11 (track 17, the catalog
                           track) in $02, a volume number of
                           $FE (254) in $03, N terminates the
                           store command, go to location $800)
```

WARNING: DOS 3.3 must be loaded in the machine before running INIT and a 48K Apple is assumed. INIT will not work with other versions of DOS or other memory sizes.

```
0800:              ORG  $800

0800:   ***********************************************************
0800:   *                                                         *
0800:   * INIT: THIS PROGRAM WILL ALLOW ITS USER TO INITIALIZE A  *
0800:   *       SINGLE TRACK WITH ANY VOLUME NUMBER DESIRED.      *
0800:   *                                                         *
0800:   * INPUT: $02 = TRACK TO BE INITIALIZED                    *
0800:   *                                                         *
0800:   *        $03 = VOLUME NUMBER                              *
0800:   *                                                         *
0800:   * ENTRY POINT: $800                                       *
0800:   *                                                         *
0800:   * PROGRAMMER: PIETER LECHNER 2/19/81                      *
0800:   *                                                         *
0800:   ***********************************************************

0800:   *          ZPAGE DEFINITIONS

0000:   PTR      EQU  $0        WORK POINTER
0002:   TRACK    EQU  $2        TRACK TO BE READ/WRITTEN
0003:   VOLUME   EQU  $3        VOLUME NUMBER
002D:   SECFND   EQU  $2D       SECTOR FOUND BY RDADR16
003E:   AA       EQU  $3E       ZPAGE CONSTANT FOR TIMING
0041:   VOL      EQU  $41       VOLUME USED BY WRADR16
0044:   TRK      EQU  $44       TRACK USED BY WRADR16
0045:   SYNCNT   EQU  $45       SYNC COUNT USED BY DSKF2
0048:   PREG     EQU  $48       MONITOR P REGISTER SAVEAREA
0087:   BELL     EQU  $87       ASCII BELL

0800:   *          OTHER ADDRESSES

03E3:   LOCRPL   EQU  $3E3      LOCATE RWTS PARMLIST SUBRTN
03D9:   RWTS     EQU  $3D9      RWTS SUBROUTINE
0578:   RTRYCNT  EQU  $578      RETRY COUNT FOR DSKF2
BB00:   NBUF1    EQU  $BB00     PRIMARY SECTOR BUFFER
BC00:   NBUF2    EQU  $BC00     SECONDARY SECTOR BUFFER
B8DC:   READ16   EQU  $B8DC     READ DATA FIELD ROUTINE
B944:   RDADR16  EQU  $B944     READ ADDRESS FIELD ROUTINE
BF0D:   DSKF2    EQU  $BF0D     FORMAT ONE TRACK ROUTINE
FDED:   COUT     EQU  $FDED     MONITOR CHARACTER OUTPUT
FDDA:   PRBYTE   EQU  $FDDA     MONITOR HEX OUTPUT

0800:   *          DISK I/O SELECTS

C080:   DRVSM0   EQU  $C080     STEP MOTOR POSITIONS
C081:   DRVSM1   EQU  $C081
C082:   DRVSM2   EQU  $C082
C083:   DRVSM3   EQU  $C083
C084:   DRVSM4   EQU  $C084
C085:   DRVSM5   EQU  $C085
C086:   DRVSM6   EQU  $C086
C087:   DRVSM7   EQU  $C087
C088:   DRVOFF   EQU  $C088     TURN DRIVE OFF AFTER 6 REVS
C089:   DRVON    EQU  $C089     TURN DRIVE ON
C08A:   DRVSL1   EQU  $C08A     SELECT DRIVE 1
C08B:   DRVSL2   EQU  $C08B     SELECT DRIVE 2

C08C:   DRVRD    EQU  $C08C     READ DATA LATCH
C08D:   DRVWR    EQU  $C08D     WRITE DATA LATCH
C08E:   DRVRDM   EQU  $C08E     SET READ MODE
C08F:   DRVWRM   EQU  $C08F     SET WRITE MODE

0800:   *          RWTS PARMLIST DEFINITION

0000:            DSECT
0000:   RPLIOB   DS   1         IOB TYPE ($01)
0001:   RPLSLT   DS   1         SLOT*16
0002:   RPLDRV   DS   1         DRIVE
0003:   RPLVOL   DS   1         VOLUME
0004:   RPLTRK   DS   1         TRACK
0005:   RPLSEC   DS   1         SECTOR
0006:   RPLDCT   DS   2         ADDRESS OF DCT
0008:   RPLBUF   DS   2         ADDRESS OF BUFFER
000A:   RPLSIZ   DS   2         SECTOR SIZE
```

```
000C:                  RPLCMD  DS   1          COMMAND CODE
0000:                  RPLCNL  EQU  $00           NULL COMMAND
0001:                  RPLCRD  EQU  $01           READ COMMAND
0002:                  RPLCWR  EQU  $02           WRITE COMMAND
0004:                  RPLCFM  EQU  $04           FORMAT COMMAND
000D:                  RPLRCD  DS   1          RETURN CODE
0010:                  RPLRWP  EQU  $10           WRITE PROTECTED
0020:                  RPLRVM  EQU  $20           VOLUME MISMATCH
0040:                  RPLRDE  EQU  $40           DRIVE ERROR
0080:                  RPLRRE  EQU  $80           READ ERROR
000E:                  RPLTVL  DS   1          TRUE VOLUME
000F:                  RPLPSL  DS   1          PREVIOUS SLOT
0010:                  RPLPDR  DS   1          PREVIOUS DRIVE
0800:                          DEND


0800:                  *       USE RWTS TO POSITION THE ARM TO THE DESIRED TRACK

0800:20 E3 03          DUMP    JSR  LOCRPL     LOCATE RWTS PARMLIST
0803:84 00                     STY  PTR        AND SAVE POINTER
0805:85 01                     STA  PTR+1

0807:A5 02                     LDA  TRACK      GET TRACK TO READ/WRITE
0809:A0 04                     LDY  #RPLTRK    STORE IN RWTS LIST
080B:91 00                     STA  (PTR),Y

080D:A9 00                     LDA  #RPLCNL    NULL OPERATION
080F:A0 0C                     LDY  #RPLCMD    AND STORE IN LIST
0811:91 00                     STA  (PTR),Y

0813:A9 00                     LDA  #0         ANY VOLUME WILL DO
0815:A0 03                     LDY  #RPLVOL
0817:91 00                     STA  (PTR),Y
0819:20 E3 03                  JSR  LOCRPL     RELOAD POINTER TO PARMS
081C:20 D9 03                  JSR  RWTS       CALL RWTS
081F:BD 89 C0                  LDA  DRVON,X    LEAVE DRIVE ON

0822:                  *       ESTABLISH ENVIRONMENT FOR DSKF2 ROUTINE

0822:A5 02                     LDA  TRACK      PASS TRACK TO DSKF2
0824:85 44                     STA  TRK

0826:A5 03                     LDA  VOLUME     AND VOLUME
0828:85 41                     STA  VOL
082A:A9 AA                     LDA  #$AA       STORE CONSTANT FOR ZPAGE..
082C:85 3E                     STA  AA         TIMING
082E:A9 28                     LDA  #$28       START WITH 40 SYNCS..
0830:85 45                     STA  SYNCNT     BETWEEN SECTORS
0832:A0 56                     LDY  #$56
0834:A9 00                     LDA  #$00
0836:99 FF BB          ZNBUF2  STA  NBUF2-1,Y ZERO SECONDARY BUFFER
0839:88                        DEY
083A:D0 FA                     BNE  ZNBUF2
083C:99 00 BB          ZNBUF1  STA  NBUF1,Y    AND PRIMARY BUFFER
083F:88                        DEY
0840:D0 FA                     BNE  ZNBUF1

0842:                  *       INITIALIZE TRACK

0842:20 0D BF                  JSR  DSKF2      FORMAT TRACK AND VERIFY
0845:A9 08                     LDA  #$08       IN CASE OF ERROR...
0847:B0 19                     BCS  HNDERR     ERROR?

0849:                  *       READ SECTOR ZERO TO VERIFY FORMATTING

0849:A9 30                     LDA  #$30       NO, DOUBLE CHECK TRACK
084B:8D 78 05                  STA  RTRYCNT    ALLOW 48 RETRIES
084E:38                NOGOOD  SEC
084F:CE 78 05                  DEC  RTRYCNT    COUNT RETRIES
0852:F0 0E                     BEQ  HNDERR
0854:20 44 B9                  JSR  RDADR16    READ AN ADDRESS FIELD
0857:B0 F5                     BCS  NOGOOD     ERROR, TRY AGAIN
0859:A5 2D                     LDA  SECFND     IS THIS SECTOR ZERO?
085B:D0 F1                     BNE  NOGOOD     NO, TRY AGAIN
```

```
085D:20 DC B8              JSR  READ16     YES, READ DATA FIELD
0860:90 1F                 BCC  DONETRK    ALL IS WELL, DONE.
0862:A0 0D        HNDERR   LDY  #RPLRCD    ELSE, PHONEY UP A RC
0864:91 00                 STA  (PTR),Y

0866:             *        ERROR OCCURED, PRINT "RC=XX"

0866:A9 87                 LDA  #BELL      BEEP THE SPEAKER
0868:20 ED FD              JSR  COUT
086B:A9 D2                 LDA  #'R        PRINT THE "RC="
086D:20 ED FD              JSR  COUT
0870:A9 C3                 LDA  #'C
0872:20 ED FD              JSR  COUT
0875:A9 BD                 LDA  #'=
0877:20 ED FD              JSR  COUT
087A:A0 0D                 LDY  #RPLRCD
087C:B1 00                 LDA  (PTR),Y    GET RWTS RETURN CODE
087E:20 DA FD              JSR  PRBYTE     PRINT RETURN CODE IN HEX

0881:             *        WHEN DONE, EXIT TO CALLER

0881:BD 88 C0     DONETRK  LDA  DRVOFF,X   TURN DRIVE OFF
0884:A9 00                 LDA  #$00
0886:85 48                 STA  PREG       CLEAR P REGISTER FOR DOS
0888:60                    RTS             ; RETURN TO CALLER
```

FTS — FIND T/S LISTS UTILITY

From time to time one of your diskettes will develop an I/O error smack in the middle of the catalog track. When this occurs, any attempt to use the diskette will result in an I/O ERROR message from DOS. Generally, when this happens, the data stored in the files on the diskette is still intact; only the pointers to the files are gone. If the data absolutely must be recovered, a knowledgeable Apple user can reconstruct the catalog from scratch. Doing this involves first finding the T/S Lists for each file, and then using ZAP to patch a catalog entry into track 17 for each file which was found. FTS is a utility which will scan a diskette for T/S Lists. Although it may flag some sectors which are not T/S Lists as being such, it will never miss a valid T/S List. Therefore, after running FTS the programmer must use ZAP to examine each track/sector printed by FTS to see if it is really a T/S List. Additionally, FTS will find every T/S List image on the diskette, even some which were for files which have since been deleted. Since it is difficult to determine which files are valid and which are old deleted files, it is usually necessary to restore all the files and copy them to another diskette, and later delete the duplicate or unwanted ones.

To run FTS, simply load the program and start execution at $900. FTS will print the track and sector number of each sector it finds which bears a resemblance to a T/S List. For example:

```
CALL -151                 (Get into the monitor from BASIC)
BLOAD FTS                 (Load the FTS program)
 ...Now insert the disk to be scanned...
900G                      (Run the FTS program on this diskette)
```

The output might look like this...

```
T=12 S=0F
T=13 S=0F
T=14 S=0D
T=14 S=0F
```

Here, only four possible files were found. ZAP should now be used to read track $12, sector $0F. At +$0C is the track and sector of the first sector in the file. This sector can be read and examined to try to identify the file and its type. Usually a BASIC program can be identified, even though it is stored in tokenized form, from the text strings contained in the PRINT statements. An ASCII conversion chart (see page 8 in the APPLE II REFERENCE MANUAL) can be used to decode these character strings. Straight T-type files will also contain ASCII text, with each line separated from the others with $8D (carriage returns). B-type files are the hardest to identify, unless the address and length stored in the first 4 bytes are recognizable. If you cannot identify the file, assume it is APPLESOFT BASIC. If this assumption turns out to be incorrect, you can always go back and ZAP the file type in the CATALOG to try something else. Given below is an example ZAP to the CATALOG to create an entry for the file whose T/S List is at T=12 S=0F.

```
CALL -151
BLOAD ZAP
 ...insert disk to be ZAPped...
800:00 N 801<800.8FEM    (Zero sector area of memory)
80B:12 0F 02             (Track 12, Sector 0F, Type-A)
:C1 A0 A0 A0 A0 A0 A0    (Name is "A")
:A0 A0 A0 A0 A0 A0 A0    (fill name out with 29 blanks)
:A0 A0 A0 A0 A0 A0 A0
:A0 A0 A0 A0 A0 A0 A0
:A0 A0
02:11 0F 02 N 900G       (Write new sector image out as
                          first (and only) catalog sector)
```

The file should immediately be copied to another diskette and then the process repeated for each T/S List found by FTS until all of the files have been recovered. As each file is recovered, it may be RENAMEd to its previous name. Once all the files have been copied to another disk, and successfully tested, the damaged disk may be re-INITialized.

```
0900:            ORG  $900

0900:     ************************************************************
0900:     *                                                          *
0900:     * FTS: THIS PROGRAM SCANS THE ENTIRE DISKETTE FOR WHAT     *
0900:     *      APPEAR TO BE TRACK/SECTOR LISTS AND PRINTS THE      *
0900:     *      TRACK AND SECTOR OF EACH ONE IT FINDS.              *
0900:     *                                                          *
0900:     * INPUT: NONE                                              *
0900:     *                                                          *
0900:     * ENTRY POINT: $900                                        *
0900:     *                                                          *
0900:     * PROGRAMMER: DON D WORTH 2/15/81                          *
0900:     *                                                          *
0900:     ************************************************************

0087:     BELL     EQU  $87       BELL CHARACTER
008D:     RETURN   EQU  $8D       CARRIAGE RETURN

0900:     *        ZPAGE DEFINITIONS

0000:     PTR      EQU  $0        WORK POINTER
003C:     A1L      EQU  $3C       MONITOR POINTER
003E:     A2L      EQU  $3E       MONITOR POINTER
0048:     PREG     EQU  $48       MONITOR STATUS REGISTER

0900:     *        OTHER ADDRESSES

0800:     BUFFER   EQU  $800      SECTOR DATA BUFFER
03E3:     LOCRPL   EQU  $3E3      LOCATE RWTS PARMLIST SUBRTN
03D9:     RWTS     EQU  $3D9      RWTS SUBROUTINE
FDED:     COUT     EQU  $FDED     PRINT ONE CHAR SUBROUTINE
FDDA:     PRBYTE   EQU  $FDDA     PRINT ONE HEX BYTE SUBRTN

0900:     *        RWTS PARMLIST DEFINITION

0000:              DSECT
0000:     RPLIOB   DS   1         IOB TYPE ($01)
0001:     RPLSLT   DS   1         SLOT*16
0002:     RPLDRV   DS   1         DRIVE
0003:     RPLVOL   DS   1         VOLUME
0004:     RPLTRK   DS   1         TRACK
0005:     RPLSEC   DS   1         SECTOR
```

```
0006:                RPLDCT  DS   2         ADDRESS OF DCT
0008:                RPLBUF  DS   2         ADDRESS OF BUFFER
000A:                RPLSIZ  DS   2         SECTOR SIZE
000C:                RPLCMD  DS   1         COMMAND CODE
0000:                RPLCNL  EQU  $00          NULL COMMAND
0001:                RPLCRD  EQU  $01          READ COMMAND
0002:                RPLCWR  EQU  $02          WRITE COMMAND
0004:                RPLCFM  EQU  $04          FORMAT COMMAND
000D:                RPLRCD  DS   1         RETURN CODE
0010:                RPLRWP  EQU  $10          WRITE PROTECTED
0020:                RPLRVM  EQU  $20          VOLUME MISMATCH
0040:                RPLRDE  EQU  $40          DRIVE ERROR
0080:                RPLRRE  EQU  $80          READ ERROR
000E:                RPLTVL  DS   1         TRUE VOLUME
000F:                RPLPSL  DS   1         PREVIOUS SLOT
0010:                RPLPDR  DS   1         PREVIOUS DRIVE
0900:                        DEND

0900:                *       START TRACK/SECTOR JUST PAST DOS (TRACK 3)

0900:20 E3 03        FTS     JSR  LOCRPL    LOCATE RWTS PARMLIST
0903:84 00                   STY  PTR       AND SAVE POINTER
0905:85 01                   STA  PTR+1

0907:A9 03                   LDA  #3        FIRST NON-DOS TRACK
0909:A0 04                   LDY  #RPLTRK   STORE IN RWTS LIST
090B:91 00                   STA  (PTR),Y

090D:A0 08                   LDY  #RPLBUF
090F:A9 00                   LDA  #>BUFFER  STORE BUFFER PTR IN LIST
0911:91 00                   STA  (PTR),Y
0913:C8                      INY
0914:A9 08                   LDA  #<BUFFER
0916:91 00                   STA  (PTR),Y

0918:A9 01                   LDA  #RPLCRD   GET COMMAND CODE FOR READ
091A:A0 0C                   LDY  #RPLCMD   AND STORE IN LIST
091C:91 00                   STA  (PTR),Y

091E:A9 00                   LDA  #0        ANY VOLUME WILL DO
0920:A0 03                   LDY  #RPLVOL
0922:91 00                   STA  (PTR),Y

0924:                *       NEW TRACK, START SECTOR AT ZERO

0924:A0 05           NEWTRK  LDY  #RPLSEC
0926:A9 00                   LDA  #0
0928:91 00                   STA  (PTR),Y

092A:                *       NOW CALL RWTS TO READ THE SECTOR

092A:20 E3 03        NEWSEC  JSR  LOCRPL    RELOAD POINTER TO PARMS
092D:20 D9 03                JSR  RWTS      CALL RWTS
0930:A9 00                   LDA  #0
0932:85 48                   STA  PREG      FIX P REG SO DOS IS HAPPY
0934:90 26                   BCC  SCAN      ALL IS WELL

0936:                *       ERROR OCCURED, PRINT "RC=XX"

0936:20 B3 09                JSR  PRTTS     PRINT TRACK/SECTOR
0939:A9 87                   LDA  #BELL     BEEP THE SPEAKER
093B:20 ED FD                JSR  COUT
093E:A9 D2                   LDA  #'R       PRINT THE "RC="
0940:20 ED FD                JSR  COUT
0943:A9 C3                   LDA  #'C
0945:20 ED FD                JSR  COUT
0948:A9 BD                   LDA  #'=
094A:20 ED FD                JSR  COUT
094D:A0 0D                   LDY  #RPLRCD
094F:B1 00                   LDA  (PTR),Y   GET RWTS RETURN CODE
```

```
0951:20 DA FD              JSR  PRBYTE     PRINT RETURN CODE IN HEX
0954:A9 8D                 LDA  #RETURN
0956:20 ED FD              JSR  COUT
0959:4C 8E 09              JMP  NXTSEC     GO ON

095C:              *       NO ERROR, SEE IF SECTOR LOOKS LIKE A T/S LIST

095C:A2 00         SCAN    LDX  #0
095E:BD 00 08      SCLP0   LDA  BUFFER,X   MAKE SURE ITS NOT ALL ZERO
0961:D0 05                 BNE  SCAN1
0963:E8                    INX
0964:D0 F8                 BNE  SCLP0
0966:F0 26                 BEQ  NXTSEC     IF IT IS, SKIP IT

0968:A2 05         SCAN1   LDX  #5         START AT OFFSET 5
096A:BD 00 08      SCLP1   LDA  BUFFER,X
096D:D0 1F                 BNE  NXTSEC     HEADER OF T/S MUST BE ZERO
096F:E8                    INX
0970:E0 0C                 CPX  #12        AT THE T/S PAIRS YET?
0972:90 F6                 BCC  SCLP1      NO, KEEP CHECKING

0974:BD 00 08      SCLP2   LDA  BUFFER,X   GET TRK
0977:C9 23                 CMP  #35        MUST BE 0-34
0979:B0 13                 BCS  NXTSEC
097B:E8                    INX
097C:BD 00 08              LDA  BUFFER,X   GET SECTOR
097F:C9 10                 CMP  #16        MUST BE 0-15
0981:B0 0B                 BCS  NXTSEC
0983:E8                    INX
0984:D0 EE                 BNE  SCLP2

0986:20 B3 09              JSR  PRTTS      ALL CONDITIONS MET
0989:A9 8D                 LDA  #RETURN
098B:20 ED FD              JSR  COUT

098E:              *       BUMP SECTOR NUMBER OR TRACK AND CONTINUE

098E:A0 05         NXTSEC  LDY  #RPLSEC
0990:B1 00                 LDA  (PTR),Y    GET LAST SECTOR
0992:18                    CLC
0993:69 01                 ADC  #1         BUMP BY ONE
0995:91 00                 STA  (PTR),Y    AND PUT IT BACK IN LIST
0997:C9 10                 CMP  #16        TOO BIG?
0999:B0 03                 BCS  NXTTRK
099B:4C 2A 09              JMP  NEWSEC     NO, GO READ IT

099E:A0 04         NXTTRK  LDY  #RPLTRK
09A0:B1 00                 LDA  (PTR),Y    GET LAST TRACK
09A2:18                    CLC
09A3:69 01                 ADC  #1         BUMF BY ONE
09A5:91 00                 STA  (PTR),Y    AND PUT IT BACK IN LIST
09A7:C9 11                 CMP  #$11       CATALOG TRACK?
09A9:F0 F3                 BEQ  NXTTRK     YES, SKIP OVER THAT ONE
09AB:C9 23                 CMP  #35        DONE ALL 35 TRACKS?
09AD:B0 03                 BCS  EXIT       YES, LEAVE
09AF:4C 24 09              JMP  NEWTRK     NO, GO READ FIRST SECTOR
09B2:60            EXIT    RTS

09B3:              *       PRTTS: PRINT "T=XX S=XX"

09B3:A9 D4         PRTTS   LDA  #'T        PRINT "T"
09B5:20 ED FD              JSR  COUT
09B8:A0 04                 LDY  #RPLTRK
09BA:B1 00                 LDA  (PTR),Y
09BC:20 CC 09              JSR  PRTEQ      PRINT "=XX "

09BF:A9 D3                 LDA  #'S        PRINT "S"
09C1:20 ED FD              JSR  COUT
09C4:A0 05                 LDY  #RPLSEC
09C6:B1 00                 LDA  (PTR),Y
09C8:20 CC 09              JSR  PRTEQ      PRINT "=XX "
09CB:60                    RTS
```

```
09CC:48             PRTEQ   PHA
09CD:A9 BD                  LDA   #'=
09CF:20 ED FD               JSR   COUT
09D2:68                     PLA
09D3:20 DA FD               JSR   PRBYTE
09D6:A9 A0                  LDA   #'
09D8:20 ED FD               JSR   COUT
09DB:60                     RTS

*** SUCCESSFUL ASSEMBLY: NO ERRORS
```

COPY — CONVERT FILES

The COPY program demonstrates the use of the DOS File Manager subroutine package from assembly language. COPY will read as input a Binary type file, stripping off the address and length information, and write the data out as a newly created Text type file. The name of the input file is assumed to be "INPUT", although this could just as easily have been inputted from the keyboard, and the name of the output file is "OUTPUT". COPY is a single drive operation, using the last drive which was referenced.

To run COPY, load it and begin execution at $800:

```
CALL -151                  (Get into the monitor from BASIC)
BLOAD COPY                 (Load the COPY program)
 ...Now insert the disk containing INPUT...
800G                       (Run the COPY program)
```

When COPY finishes, it will return to BASIC. If any errors occur, the return code passed back from the File Manager will be printed. Consult the documentation on the File Manager parameter list in Chapter 6 for a list of these return codes.

```
0800:              ORG  $800

0800:            *************************************************************
0800:            *                                                           *
0800:            * COPY:THIS PROGRAM DEMONSTRATES THE USE OF THE DOS FILE    *
0800:            *      MANAGER BY COPYING A BINARY FILE TO A TEXT FILE.     *
0800:            *                                                           *
0800:            * INPUT: INPUT FILE NAME IS "INPUT"                         *
0800:            *        OUTPUT FILE NAME IS "OUTPUT"                       *
0800:            *                                                           *
0800:            * ENTRY POINT: $800                                         *
0800:            *                                                           *
0800:            * PROGRAMMER: DON D WORTH 2/19/81                           *
0800:            *                                                           *
0800:            *************************************************************

0087:            BELL     EQU  $87          BELL CHARACTER

0800:            *        ZPAGE DEFINITIONS

0000:            PTR      EQU  $0           WORK POINTER
0002:            BUFP     EQU  $2           BUFFER POINTER
0004:            EBYTE    EQU  $4
003C:            A1L      EQU  $3C          MONITOR POINTER
003E:            A2L      EQU  $3E          MONITOR POINTER

0800:            *        OTHER ADDRESSES

1000:            BUFFER   EQU  $1000        DATA BUFFER
03D0:            DOSWRM   EQU  $3D0         DOS WARMSTART ADDRESS
03E3:            LOCRPL   EQU  $3E3         LOCATE RWTS PARMLIST SUBRTN
03DC:            LOCFPL   EQU  $3DC         LOCATE FILE MGR PARMLIST SUB
03D6:            FM       EQU  $3D6         FILE MANAGER ENTRY POINT
FDED:            COUT     EQU  $FDED        PRINT ONE CHAR SUBROUTINE
FDDA:            PRBYTE   EQU  $FDDA        PRINT ONE HEX BYTE SUBRTN

0800:            *        FILE MANAGER PARMLIST DEFINITION

0000:                     DSECT
0000:            FMOCOD   DS   1            OPERATION CODE
0001:            FMOCOP   EQU  $01             OPEN
0002:            FMOCCL   EQU  $02             CLOSE
0003:            FMOCRD   EQU  $03             READ
0004:            FMOCWR   EQU  $04             WRITE
0005:            FMOCDE   EQU  $05             DELETE
0006:            FMOCCA   EQU  $06             CATALOG
0007:            FMOCLO   EQU  $07             LOCK
0008:            FMOCUN   EQU  $08             UNLOCK
0009:            FMOCRE   EQU  $09             RENAME
000A:            FMOCPO   EQU  $0A             POSITION
000B:            FMOCIN   EQU  $0B             INIT
000C:            FMOCVE   EQU  $0C             VERIFY
0001:            FMSBCD   DS   1            SUBCODE
0000:            FMSBNO   EQU  $00             NO OPERATION
0001:            FMSBON   EQU  $01             READ/WRITE ONE BYTE
0002:            FMSBRA   EQU  $02             READ/WRITE RANGE OF BYTES
0003:            FMSBPO   EQU  $03             POSITION AND DO ONE BYTE
0004:            FMSBPR   EQU  $04             POSITION AND DO RANGE
0002:            FMPRMS   DS   8            SPECIFIC PARAMETERS

000A:            *        OPEN PARMS
0002:                     ORG  FMPRMS
0002:            FMRCLN   DS   2            RECORD LENGTH
0004:            FMVOL    DS   1            VOLUME
0005:            FMDRV    DS   1            DRIVE
0006:            FMSLT    DS   1            SLOT
0007:            FMTYPE   DS   1            TYPE
0000:            FMTYPT   EQU  0               TEXT
0001:            FMTYPI   EQU  1               INTEGER
0002:            FMTYPA   EQU  2               APPLESOFT
0004:            FMTYPB   EQU  4               BINARY
0008:            FMNAME   DS   2            ADDRESS OF FILE NAME
```

```
000A:              *         READ/WRITE PARMS
0002:                        ORG  FMPRMS
0002:              FMRCNM    DS   2          RECORD NUMBER
0004:              FMOFFS    DS   2          BYTE OFFSET
0006:              FMRALN    DS   2          RANGE LENGTH
0008:              FMRAAD    DS   2          RANGE ADDRESS
0008:              FMDATA    EQU  FMRAAD     DATA BYTE READ/WRITTEN

000A:              *         RENAME PARMS
0002:                        ORG  FMPRMS
0002:              FMNNAM    DS   2          ADDRESS OF NEW NAME

0004:              *         INIT PARMS
0002:                        ORG  FMPRMS
0001:              FMPAGE    EQU  FMSBCD     FIRST PAGE OF DOS IMAGE

0002:              *         COMMON PARMS
000A:                        ORG  FMPRMS+8
000A:              FMRC      DS   1          RETURN CODE
0000:              FMRCOK    EQU  0             NO ERRORS
0002:              FMRCBO    EQU  2             BAD OPCODE
0003:              FMRCBS    EQU  3             BAD SUBCODE
0004:              FMRCWP    EQU  4             WRITE PROTECTED
0005:              FMRCED    EQU  5             END OF DATA
0006:              FMRCNF    EQU  6             FILE NOT FOUND
0007:              FMRCBV    EQU  7             BAD VOLUME
0008:              FMRCIO    EQU  8             I/O ERROR
0009:              FMRCDF    EQU  9             DISK FULL
000A:              FMRCLK    EQU  10            FILE LOCKED
000B:                        DS   1          NOT USED
000C:              FMFMWA    DS   2          FILE MANAGER WORKAREA PTR
000E:              FMTSL     DS   2          T/S LIST PTR
0010:              FMBUFF    DS   2          DATA BUFFER PTR
0800:                        DEND

0800:              *         LOCATE FM PARMLIST

0800:20 DC 03      COPY      JSR  LOCFPL     FIND PARMLIST
0803:84 00                   STY  PTR        SET UP POINTER TO IT
0805:85 01                   STA  PTR+1

0807:              *         OPEN INPUT FILE

0807:A0 08                   LDY  #FMNAME    STORE INPUT FILE NAME
0809:A9 AC                   LDA  #>INAME    PTR IN LIST
080B:91 00                   STA  (PTR),Y
080D:C8                      INY
080E:A9 09                   LDA  #<INAME
0810:91 00                   STA  (PTR),Y
0812:A0 07                   LDY  #FMTYPE    BINARY FILE AS INPUT
0814:A9 04                   LDA  #FMTYPB
0816:91 00                   STA  (PTR),Y
0818:A2 01                   LDX  #1         OLD FILE EXPECTED
081A:20 D3 08                JSR  OPEN       AND OPEN THE FILE
081D:90 03                   BCC  INOP
081F:4C BC 08                JMP  ERROR      ANY ERROR IS FATAL

0822:A5 02         INOP      LDA  BUFP
0824:8D EA 09                STA  IBUFF      SAVE OPEN FILE BUFFER
0827:A5 03                   LDA  BUFP+1
0829:8D EB 09                STA  IBUFF+1
082C:20 5A 09                JSR  REWIND     POSITION TO START OF FILE
```

```
082F:                 *        OPEN OUTPUT FILE

082F:A0 08                     LDY  #FMNAME   STORE OUTPUT FILE NAME
0831:A9 CA                     LDA  #>ONAME   PTR IN LIST
0833:91 00                     STA  (PTR),Y
0835:C8                        INY
0836:A9 09                     LDA  #<ONAME
0838:91 00                     STA  (PTR),Y
083A:A0 07                     LDY  #FMTYPE   TEXT FILE AS OUTPUT
083C:A9 00                     LDA  #FMTYPT
083E:91 00                     STA  (PTR),Y
0840:A2 00                     LDX  #0        NEW FILE IS OK
0842:20 D3 08                  JSR  OPEN
0845:90 0B                     BCC  OUTOP
0847:A0 0A                     LDY  #FMRC
0849:B1 00                     LDA  (PTR),Y
084B:C9 06                     CMP  #FMRCNF   FILE NOT FOUND?
084D:F0 03                     BEQ  OUTOP     YES, WAS ALLOCATED THEN
084F:4C BC 08                  JMP  ERROR

0852:A5 02            OUTOP    LDA  BUFP      SAVE OPEN OUTPUT FILE BUFFER
0854:8D E8 09                  STA  OBUFF
0857:A5 03                     LDA  BUFP+1
0859:8D E9 09                  STA  OBUFF+1
085C:20 5A 09                  JSR  REWIND    POSITION TO START OF FILE

085F:                 *        READ ADDRESS/LENGTH FROM BINARY FILE

085F:A9 04                     LDA  #4        READ 4 BYTES FIRST
0861:A0 06                     LDY  #FMRALN
0863:91 00                     STA  (PTR),Y
0865:A9 00                     LDA  #0
0867:C8                        INY
0868:91 00                     STA  (PTR),Y
086A:20 74 09                  JSR  READ

086D:                 *        READ ENTIRE BINARY FILE INTO MEMORY AT $1000

086D:AD 02 10                  LDA  BUFFER+2  COPY DATA LENGTH TO LIST
0870:A0 06                     LDY  #FMRALN
0872:91 00                     STA  (PTR),Y
0874:AD 03 10                  LDA  BUFFER+3
0877:C8                        INY
0878:91 00                     STA  (PTR),Y
087A:18                        CLC
087B:AD 02 10                  LDA  BUFFER+2  COMPUTE ENDING BYTE
087E:48                        PHA
087F:69 00                     ADC  #>BUFFER
0881:85 04                     STA  EBYTE
0883:AD 03 10                  LDA  BUFFER+3
0886:48                        PHA
0887:69 10                     ADC  #<BUFFER
0889:85 05                     STA  EBYTE+1
088B:20 74 09                  JSR  READ      READ BLOB INTO MEMORY

088E:                 *        WRITE ENTIRE BLOB OUT INTO TEXT FILE

088E:A0 00                     LDY  #0
0890:98                        TYA
0891:91 04                     STA  (EBYTE),Y MARK END OF FILE
0893:68                        PLA
0894:A0 07                     LDY  #FMRALN+1 SET RANGE LENGTH
0896:91 00                     STA  (PTR),Y
0898:88                        DEY
0899:68                        PLA
089A:91 00                     STA  (PTR),Y
089C:20 82 09                  JSR  WRITE     WRITE BLOB FROM MEMORY
```

```
089F:                *         WHEN FINISHED, CLOSE FILES

089F:AD E8 09        EXIT      LDA   OBUFF
08A2:85 02                     STA   BUFP
08A4:AD E9 09                  LDA   OBUFF+1
08A7:85 03                     STA   BUFP+1
08A9:20 46 09                  JSR   CLOSE       CLOSE OUTPUT FILE
08AC:AD EA 09                  LDA   IBUFF
08AF:85 02                     STA   BUFP
08B1:AD EB 09                  LDA   IBUFF+1
08B4:85 03                     STA   BUFP+1
08B6:20 46 09                  JSR   CLOSE       CLOSE INPUT FILE
08B9:4C D0 03                  JMP   DOSWRM      BACK TO DOS

08BC:                *         ERROR, PRINT "ERRXX"

08BC:A0 0A           ERROR     LDY   #FMRC       FIND RETURN CODE
08BE:B1 00                     LDA   (PTR),Y
08C0:48                        PHA
08C1:A9 C5           ERR       LDA   #'E         PRINT "ERR"
08C3:20 ED FD                  JSR   COUT
08C6:A9 D2                     LDA   #'R
08C8:20 ED FD                  JSR   COUT
08CB:20 ED FD                  JSR   COUT
08CE:68                        PLA
08CF:20 DA FD                  JSR   PRBYTE      PRINT HEX CODE
08D2:00                        BRK                DIE HORRIBLY

08D3:                *         OPEN: COMPLETE PARMLIST AND OPEN FILE

08D3:AD D2 03        OPEN      LDA   DOSWRM+2    FIND DOS ENTRY
08D6:85 03                     STA   BUFP+1
08D8:A0 00                     LDY   #0
08DA:84 02                     STY   BUFP        POINT AT BUFFER CHAIN

08DC:                *         SCAN DOS BUFFERS FOR A FREE ONE

08DC:B1 02           GBUF0     LDA   (BUFP),Y    LOCATE NEXT DOS BUFFER
08DE:48                        PHA
08DF:C8                        INY
08E0:B1 02                     LDA   (BUFP),Y
08E2:85 03                     STA   BUFP+1
08E4:68                        PLA
08E5:85 02                     STA   BUFP
08E7:D0 0A                     BNE   GBUF        GOT ONE
08E9:A5 03                     LDA   BUFP+1
08EB:D0 06                     BNE   GBUF        GOT ONE

08ED:A9 0C                     LDA   #12         NO FILE BUFFERS RETURN CODE
08EF:48                        PHA
08F0:4C C1 08                  JMP   ERR         GO PRINT MESSAGE

08F3:A0 00           GBUF      LDY   #0          LOOK AT FILENAME
08F5:B1 02                     LDA   (BUFP),Y
08F7:F0 04                     BEQ   GOTBUF      NONE THERE, FREE BUFFER
08F9:A0 24                     LDY   #36         IT'S NOT FREE
08FB:D0 DF                     BNE   GBUF0       GO GET NEXT ONE

08FD:A9 01           GOTBUF    LDA   #1
08FF:91 02                     STA   (BUFP),Y    MARK BUFFER IN USE

0901:                *         FINISH COMPLETING OPEN LIST

0901:A0 00                     LDY   #FMOCOD
0903:A9 01                     LDA   #FMOCOP
0905:91 00                     STA   (PTR),Y     SET OPCODE TO OPEN
0907:A9 00                     LDA   #0
0909:A0 02                     LDY   #FMRCLN
090B:91 00                     STA   (PTR),Y     SET RECORD LENGTH TO 0
090D:C8                        INY
090E:91 00                     STA   (PTR),Y
0910:A0 04                     LDY   #FMVOL
0912:91 00                     STA   (PTR),Y     AND VOLUME (ANY VOL)
```

```
0914:20 E3 03            JSR  LOCRPL     FIND RWTS PARMS
0917:84 3C               STY  A1L
0919:85 3D               STA  A1L+1
091B:A0 01               LDY  #1
091D:B1 3C               LDA  (A1L),Y    GET SLOT*16
091F:4A                  LSR  A
0920:4A                  LSR  A
0921:4A                  LSR  A
0922:4A                  LSR  A          SLOT=SLOT/16
0923:A0 06               LDY  #FMSLT
0925:91 00               STA  (PTR),Y    STORE IN LIST
0927:A0 02               LDY  #2
0929:B1 3C               LDA  (A1L),Y    GET DRIVE
092B:A0 05               LDY  #FMDRV
092D:91 00               STA  (PTR),Y    AND SLOT

092F:           *        COMMON INTERFACE TO FILE MANAGER

092F:A0 1E      CALLFM   LDY  #30
0931:B1 02      CFMLP1   LDA  (BUFP),Y   GET THREE BUFFER PTRS
0933:48                  PHA
0934:C8                  INY
0935:C0 24               CPY  #36
0937:90 F8               BCC  CFMLP1

0939:A0 11               LDY  #FMBUFF+1
093B:68         CFMLP2   PLA
093C:91 00               STA  (PTR),Y    COPY THEM TO FM LIST
093E:88                  DEY
093F:C0 0C               CPY  #FMFMWA
0941:B0 F8               BCS  CFMLP2

0943:4C D6 03            JMP  FM         EXIT THRU FILE MANAGER

0946:           *        CLOSE: CLOSE DOS FILE

0946:A0 00      CLOSE    LDY  #FMOCOD
0948:A9 02               LDA  #FMOCCL
094A:91 00               STA  (PTR),Y
094C:20 2F 09            JSR  CALLFM     CLOSE FILE
094F:90 03               BCC  CLOK
0951:4C BC 08            JMP  ERROR
0954:A0 00      CLOK     LDY  #0         FREE BUFFER
0956:98                  TYA
0957:91 02               STA  (BUFP),Y
0959:60                  RTS

095A:           *        REWIND: POSITION TO START OF FILE

095A:A0 02      REWIND   LDY  #FMRCNM
095C:A9 00               LDA  #0
095E:91 00      REWLP    STA  (PTR),Y    ZERO RECORD NUMBER AND..
0960:C8                  INY
0961:C0 06               CPY  #FMOFFS+2 BYTE OFFSET.
0963:90 F9               BCC  REWLP
0965:A0 00               LDY  #FMOCOD
0967:A9 0A               LDA  #FMOCPO    POSITION OPCODE
0969:91 00               STA  (PTR),Y
096B:20 2F 09            JSR  CALLFM     EXIT VIA FILE MANAGER
096E:90 03               BCC  REWRTS     CHECK FOR ERRORS
0970:4C BC 08            JMP  ERROR
0973:60         REWRTS   RTS
```

```
0974:               *          READ: READ A RANGE OF BYTES TO $1000

0974:AD EA 09       READ       LDA  IBUFF      FIND PROPER BUFFER
0977:85 02                     STA  BUFP
0979:AD EB 09                  LDA  IBUFF+1
097C:85 03                     STA  BUFP+1
097E:A9 03                     LDA  #FMOCRD    READ OPCODE
0980:D0 0C                     BNE  DOIO       GO DO COMMON CODE

0982:               *          WRITE: WRITE A RANGE OF BYTES FROM $1000

0982:AD E8 09       WRITE      LDA  OBUFF      FIND PROPER BUFFER
0985:85 02                     STA  BUFP
0987:AD E9 09                  LDA  OBUFF+1
098A:85 03                     STA  BUFP+1
098C:A9 04                     LDA  #FMOCWR    WRITE OPCODE
098E:               *          BNE     DOIO

098E:               *          DOIO: READ/WRITE A RANGE OF BYTES

098E:A0 00          DOIO       LDY  #FMOCOD
0990:91 00                     STA  (PTR),Y    SET OPCODE
0992:A0 01                     LDY  #FMSBCD
0994:A9 02                     LDA  #FMSBRA
0996:91 00                     STA  (PTR),Y    DO RANGE OF BYTES
0998:A0 08                     LDY  #FMRAAD
099A:A9 00                     LDA  #>BUFFER
099C:91 00                     STA  (PTR),Y    RANGE ADDRESS=$1000
099E:C8                        INY
099F:A9 10                     LDA  #<BUFFER
09A1:91 00                     STA  (PTR),Y
09A3:20 2F 09                  JSR  CALLFM     CALL FM TO DO I/O OPERATION
09A6:90 03                     BCC  DOIORT
09A8:4C BC 08                  JMP  ERROR
09AB:60             DOIORT     RTS

09AC:               *          DATA

09AC:C9 CE D0       INAME      ASC  'INPUT
09AF:D5 D4 A0
09B2:A0 A0 A0
09B5:A0 A0 A0
09B8:A0 A0 A0
09BB:A0 A0 A0
09BE:A0 A0 A0
09C1:A0 A0 A0
09C4:A0 A0 A0
09C7:A0 A0 A0
09CA:CF D5 D4       ONAME      ASC  'OUTPUT
09CD:D0 D5 D4
09D0:A0 A0 A0
09D3:A0 A0 A0
09D6:A0 A0 A0
09D9:A0 A0 A0
09DC:A0 A0 A0
09DF:A0 A0 A0
09E2:A0 A0 A0
09E5:A0 A0 A0

09E8:               OBUFF      DS   2
09EA:               IBUFF      DS   2

*** SUCCESSFUL ASSEMBLY: NO ERRORS
```

APPENDIX B
DISK PROTECTION SCHEMES

As the quantity and quality of Apple II software has increased, so has the incidence of illegal duplication of copyrighted software. To combat this, software vendors have introduced methods for protecting their software. Since most protection schemes involve a modified or custom Disk Operating System, it seems appropriate to discuss disk protection in general.

Typically, a protection scheme's purpose is to stop unauthorized duplication of the contents of the diskette, although it may also include, or be limited to, preventing the listing of the software (if it is in BASIC). This has been attempted in a variety of ways, all of which necessitate reading and writing non-standard formats on the disk. If the reader is unclear about how a normal diskette is formatted, he should refer to Chapter 3 for more information.

Early protection methods were primitive in comparison to what is being done now. Just as the methods of protection have improved, so have the techniques people have used to break them. The cycle seems endless. As new and more sophisticated schemes are developed, they are soon broken, prompting the software vendor to try to create even more sophisticated systems.

It seems reasonable at this time to say that it is impossible to protect a disk in such a way that it can't be broken. This is, in large part, due to the fact that the diskette must be "bootable"; i.e. that it must contain at least one sector (Track 0, Sector 0) which can be read by the program in the PROM on the disk controller card. This means that it is possible to trace the boot process by disassembling the normal sector or sectors that must be on the disk. It turns out that it is even possible to protect these sectors. Because of a lack of space on the PROM (256 bytes), the software doesn't fully check either the Address Field or the Data Field. But potential protection schemes which take advantage of this are limited and must involve only certain changes which will be discussed below.

Most protected disks use a modified version of Apple's DOS. This is a much easier task than writing one's own Disk Operating System and will be the primary area covered by this discussion.

Although there are a vast array of different protection schemes, they all consist of having some portion of the disk unreadable by a normal Disk Operating System. The two logical areas to alter are the Address Field and the Data Field. Each include a number of bytes which, if changed, will cause a sector to be unreadable. We will examine how that is done in some detail.

The Address Field normally starts with the bytes $D5/$AA/$96. If any one of these bytes were changed, DOS would not be able to locate that particular Address Field, causing an error. While all three bytes can and have been changed by various schemes, it is important to remember that they must be chosen in such a way as to guarantee their uniqueness. Apple's DOS does this by reserving the bytes $D5 and $AA; i.e. these bytes are not used in the storage of data. The sequence chosen by the would-be disk protector can not occur anywhere else on the track, other than in another Address Field. Next comes the address information itself (volume, track, sector, and checksum). Some common techniques include changing the order of the information, doubling the sector numbers, or altering the checksum with some constant. Any of the above would cause an I/O error in a normal DOS. Finally, we have the two closing bytes ($DE/$AA), which are similar to the starting bytes, but with a difference. Their uniqueness is not critical, since DOS will read whatever two bytes follow the information field, using them for verification, but not to locate the field itself.

The Data Field is quite similar to the Address Field in that its three parts correspond almost identically, as far as protection schemes are concerned. The Data Field starts with $D5/$AA/$AD, only the third byte being different, and all that applies to the Address Field applies here also. Switching the third bytes between the two fields is an example of a protective measure. The data portion consists of 342 bytes of data, followed by a checksum byte. Quite often the data is written so that the checksum computation will be non-zero, causing an error. The closing bytes are identical to those of the Address Field ($DE/$AA).

As mentioned earlier, the PROM on the disk controller skips certain parts of both types of fields. In particular, neither trailing byte ($DE/$AA) is read or verified nor is the checksum tested, allowing these bytes to be modified even in track 0 sector 0. However, this protection is easily defeated by making slight modifications to DOS's RWTS routines, rendering it unreliable as a protective measure.

In the early days of disk protection, a single alteration was all that was needed to stop all but a few from copying the disk. Now, with more educated users and powerful utilities available, multiple schemes are quite commonly used. The first means of protection was probably that of hidden control characters imbedded in a file name. Now it is common to find a disk using multiple non-standard formats written even <u>between</u> tracks.

A state of the art protection scheme consists of two elements. First, the data is stored on the diskette in some non-standard way in order to make copying very difficult. Secondly, some portion of memory is utilized that will be altered upon a RESET. (For example, the primary text page or certain zero page locations) This is to prevent the software from being removed from memory intact.

THE RACE IS ON BETWEEN THE PROTECTORS AND THE UNPROTECTORS.

Recently, several "nibble" or byte copy programs have become available. Unlike traditional copy programs which require the data to be in a predefined format, these utilities make as few assumptions as possible about the data structure. Ever since protected disks were first introduced, it has been asked, "why can't a track be read into memory and then written back out to another diskette in exactly the same way?". The problem lies with the self-sync or auto-sync bytes. (For a full discussion see Chapter 3) These bytes contain extra zero bits that are lost when read into memory. In memory it is impossible to determine the difference between a hexadecimal $FF that was data and a hex $FF that was a self-sync byte. Two solutions are currently being implemented in nibble copy programs. One is to analyze the data on a track with the hope that the sync gaps can be located by deduction. This has a high probability of success if 13 or 16 sectors are present, even if they have been modified, but may not be effective in dealing with non-standard sectoring where sectors are larger than 256 bytes. In short, this method is effective but by no means foolproof. The second method is simple but likewise has a difficulty. It simply writes every hex $FF found on the track as if it were a sync byte. This, however, will expand the physical space needed to write the track back out, since sync bytes require 25% more room. If enough hex $FF's occur in the data, the track will overwrite itself. This can happen in general if the drive used to write the data is significantly slower than normal. Thus, we are back to having to analyze the data and, in effect, make some assumptions. It appears that, apart from using some hardware device to help find the sync bytes, a software program must make some assumptions about how the data is structured on the diskette.

The result of the introduction of nibble copy programs has been to "force the hand" of the software vendors. The initial response was to develop new protection schemes that defeated the nibble copy programs. More recent protection schemes, however, involve hardware and timing dependencies which require current nibble copy programs to rely heavily upon the user for direction. If the present trend continues, it is very likely that protection schemes will evolve to a point where automated techniques cannot be used to defeat them.

APPENDIX C
GLOSSARY

ACCESS TIME	The time required to locate and read or write data on a direct access storage device, such as a diskette drive.
ADDRESS	The numeric location of a piece of data in memory. Usually given as a hexadecimal number from $0000 to $FFFF (65535 decimal). A disk address is the location of a data sector, expressed in terms of its track and sector numbers.
ALGORITHM	A sequence of steps which may be performed by a program or other process, which will produce a given result.
ALPHANUMERIC	An alphabetic character (A-Z) or a numeric digit (0-9). The term used to refer to the class of all characters and digits.
ANALOG	As opposed to digital. Having a value which is continuous, such as a voltage or electrical resistance.
AND	The logical process of determining whether two bits are both ones. 0 AND 1 results in 0 (false), 1 AND 1 results in 1 (true).
ARM	The portion of a disk drive which suspends the read/write head over the disk's surface. The arm can be moved radially to allow access to different tracks.
ASCII	American Standard Code for Information Interchange. A hexadecimal to character conversion code assignment, such that the 256 possible values of a single byte may each represent a alphabetic, numeric, special, or control character. ASCII is used when interfacing to peripherals, such as keyboards, printers, or video text displays.

ASSEMBLY LANGUAGE — Also known as MACHINE LANGUAGE. The native programming language of the individual computer. Assembly language is oriented to the machine, and is not humanized, as is BASIC, PASCAL, or FORTRAN. An assembler is used to convert assembly language statements to an executable program.

BACKUP — The process of making a copy of a program or data against the possibility of its accidental loss or destruction.

BASE — The number system in use. Decimal is base 10, since each digit represents a power of 10 (1,10,100,...). Hexadecimal is base 16 (1,16,256,...). Binary is base 2 (1,2,4,8,...).

BINARY — A number system based upon powers of 2. Only the digits 0 and 1 are used. 101 in binary, for example, is 1 units digit, 0 twos, and 1 fours, or 5 in decimal.

BIT — A single binary digit (a 1 or a 0). A bit is the smallest unit of storage or information in a computer.

BIT CELL — The space on a diskette, between two clock pulses, which can hold the value of a single binary 0 or 1 (bit).

BIT SLIP MARKS — The epilogue of a disk field. Used to double check that the disk head is still in read sync and the sector has not been damaged.

BOOT/BOOTSTRAP — The process of loading a very large program into memory by loading successively larger pieces, each of which loads its successor. The program loads itself by "pulling itself up by its bootstraps".

BRK — BREAK. An assembly langauge instruction which can be used to force an interrupt and immediate suspension of execution of a program.

BUFFER — An area of memory used to temporarily hold data as it is being transferred to or from a peripheral, such as a disk drive.

BUG — A programming error. Faulty operation of a program.

BYTE	The smallest unit of addressable memory in a computer. A byte usually consists of 8 bits and can contain a decimal number ranging from 0 to 255 or a single alphanumeric character.
CARRIAGE RETURN	A control character which instructs the printer to end one line and begin another. When printing a carriage return is usually followed by a line feed.
CARRY FLAG	A 6502 processor flag which indicates that a previous addition resulted in a carry. Also used as an error indicator by many system programs.
CATALOG	A directory of the files on a diskette. See DIRECTORY.
CHAIN	A linked list of data elements. Data is chained if its elements need not be contiguous in storage and each element can be found from its predecessor via an address pointer.
CHECKSUM/CRC	A method for verifying that data has not been damaged. When data is written, the sum of all its constituent bytes is stored with it. If, when the data is later read, its sum no longer matches the checksum, it has been damaged.
CLOBBERED	Damaged or destroyed. A clobbered sector is one which has been overwritten such that it is unrecoverable.
CODE	Executable instructions to the computer, usually in machine language.
COLDSTART	A restart of a program which reinitializes all of its parameters, usually erasing any work which was in progress at the time of the restart. A DOS coldstart erases the BASIC program in memory.
CONTIGUOUS	Physically next to. Two bytes are contiguous if they are adjoining each other in memory or on the disk.
CONTROL BLOCK	A collection of data which is used by the operating system to manage resources. Examples of a control block used by DOS are the file buffers.

CONTROL CHARACTER	A special ASCII code which is used to perform a unique function on a peripheral, but does not generate a printable character. Carriage return, line feed, form feed, and bell are all control characters.
CONTROLLER CARD	A hardware circuit board which is plugged into an APPLE connector which allows communication with a peripheral device, such as a disk or printer. A controller card usually contains a small driver program in ROM.
CSWL	A vector in zero-page through which output data is passed for display on the CRT or for printing.
CYCLE	The smallest unit of time within the central processor of the computer. Each machine language instruction requires two or more cycles to complete. One cycle (on the APPLE) is one micro-second or one millionth of a second.
DATA	Units of information.
DATA SECTOR BUFFER	On the APPLE, a 256 byte buffer used by DOS to hold the image of any given sector on the diskette. As information is read from the file, data is extracted from the data sector buffer until it is exhausted, at which time it is refilled with the next sector image.
DATA TYPE	The type of information stored in a byte. A byte might contain a printable ASCII character, binary numeric data, or a machine language instruction.
DCT	Device Characteristics Table. Used as an input parameter table to Read/Write Track/Sector (RWTS) to describe the hardware characteristics of the diskette drive.
DECIMAL	A number system based upon powers of 10. Digits range from 0 to 9.
DEFERRED COMMANDS	DOS commands which may (or must) be invoked from within an executing BASIC program. OPEN, READ, WRITE, and CLOSE are all examples of deferred commands.

DIGITAL	As opposed to analog. Discrete values as opposed to continuous ones. Only digital values may be stored in a computer. Analog measurements from the real world, such as a voltage or the level of light outside, must be converted into a numerical value which, of necessity, must be "rounded off" to a discrete value.
DIRECT ACCESS	Peripheral storage allowing rapid access of any piece of data, regardless of its placement on the medium. Magnetic tape is generally not considered direct access, since the entire tape must be read to locate the last byte. A diskette is direct access, since the arm may be rapidly moved to any track and sector.
DIRECTORY	A catalog of all files stored on a diskette. The directory must contain each file's name and its location on the disk as well as other information regarding the type of data stored there.
DISK INITIALIZATION	The process which places track formatting information, including sectors and gaps, on a blank diskette. During disk initialization, DOS also places a VTOC and directory on the newly formatted disk, as well as saving the HELLO program.
DISPLACEMENT	The distance from the beginning of a block of data to a particular byte or field. Displacements are usually given beginning with 0, for the first byte, 1 for the second, etc. Also known as an offset.
DRIVER	A program which provides an input stream to another program or an output device. A printer driver accepts input from a user program in the form of lines to be printed, and sends them to the printer.
DUMP	An unformatted or partially formatted listing of the contents of memory or a diskette in hexadecimal. Used for diagnostic purposes.
ENCODE	To translate data from one form to another for any of a number of reasons. In DOS 3.3, Data is encoded from 8 bit bytes to 6 bit bytes for storage on a DISK II.

ENTRY POINT (EPA)	The entry point address is the location within a program where execution is to start. This is not necessarily the same as the load point (or lowest memory address in the program).
EOF	End Of File. This mark signals the end of a data file. $00 for APPLE DOS text files.
EPILOGUE	The last three bytes of a field on a track. These unique bytes are used to insure the integrity of the data which preceeds them.
EXCLUSIVE OR	A logical operation which compares two bits to determine if they are different. 1 EOR 0 results in 1. 1 EOR 1 results in 0.
FIELD	A group of contiguous bytes forming a single piece of data, such as a person's name, his age, or his social security number. In disk formatting, a group of data bytes surrounded by gaps.
FILE	A named collection of data on a diskette or other mass storage medium. Files can contain data or programs.
FILE BUFFERS	In APPLE DOS, a collection of buffers used to manage one open file. Included are a data sector buffer, a Track/Sector List sector buffer, a file manager workarea buffer, the name of the file, and pointers. The DOS command, MAXFILES 3, causes 3 of these file buffers to be allocated.
FILE DESCRIPTOR	A single entry in a diskette directory which describes one file. Included are the name of the file, its data type, its length, and its location on the diskette.
FILE MANAGER	That portion of DOS which manages files. The file manager handles such general operations as OPEN, CLOSE, READ, WRITE, POSITION, RENAME, DELETE, etc.
FILE TYPE	The type of data held by a file. Valid DOS file types are Binary, Applesoft, Integer-BASIC, Text, Relocatable, S, A, and B.
FIRMWARE	A middle ground between hardware and software. Usually used to describe micro-code or programs which have been stored in read-only memory.

GAPS	The spaces between fields of data on a diskette. Gaps on an APPLE diskette contain self-sync bytes.
HARD ERROR	An unrecoverable Input/Output error. The data stored in the disk sector can never be successfully read again.
HARDWARE	Physical computer equipment, as opposed to programs which run on the equipment. A disk drive is an example of a hardware component.
HEAD	The read/write head on a diskette drive. A magnetic pickup, similar in nature to the head on a stereo tapedeck, which rests on the spinning surface of the diskette.
HEXADECIMAL/HEX	A numeric system based on powers of 16. Valid hex digits range from 0 to 9 and A to F, where A is 10, B is 11, ... , and F is 15. B30 is 11 256's, 3 16's, and 0 1's, or 2864 in decimal. Two hexadecimal digits can be used to represent the contents of one byte. Hexadecimal is used with computers because it easily converts with binary.
HIGH MEMORY	Those memory locations which have high address values. $FFFF is the highest memory location. Also called the "top" of memory.
HIMEM	APPLE's zero-page address which identifies the first byte past the available memory which can be used to store BASIC programs and their variables.
IMMEDIATE COMMAND	A DOS command which may be entered at any time, especially when DOS is waiting for a command from the keyboard. Deferred commands are the opposite of immediate commands.
INDEX	A displacement into a table or block of storage.
INSTRUCTION	A single step to be performed in an assembly language or machine language program. Instructions perform such operations as addition, subtraction, store, or load.
INTEGER	As opposed to floating point. A "whole" number with no fraction associated with it.

INTERCEPT — A program which logically places itself in the execution path of another program, or pair of programs. A video intercept is used to re-direct program output from the screen to a printer, for example.

INTERLEAVE — The practice of selecting the order of sectors on a diskette track to minimize access time due to rotational delay. Also called "skewing" or interlacing.

INTERRUPT — A hardware signal which causes the computer to halt execution of a program and enter a special handler routine. Interrupts are used to service real-time clock time-outs, BRK instructions, and RESET.

IOB — Input/Output Block. A collection of parameter data, passed to Read/Write Track/Sector, describing the operation to be performed.

I/O ERROR — Input/Output Error. An error which occurs during transmission of data to or from a peripheral device, such as a disk or cassette tape.

JMP — A 6502 assembly langauge instruction which causes the computer to begin executing instructions at a different location in memory. Similar to a GOTO statement in BASIC.

JSR — A 6502 assembly langauge instruction which causes the computer to "call" a subroutine. Similar to a GOSUB statement in BASIC.

K — A unit of measurement, usually applied to bytes. 1 K bytes is equivalent to 1024 bytes.

KSWL — A vector in zero-page through which input data is passed from the keyboard or a remote terminal.

LABEL — A name associated with a location in a program or in memory. Labels are used in assembly langauge much like statement numbers are used in BASIC.

LATCH — A component into which the Input/Output hardware can store a byte value, which will hold that value until the central processor has time to read it (or vice versa).

LINK	An address pointer in an element of a linked chain of data or buffers.
LIST	A one dimensional sequential array of data items.
LOAD POINT (LP)	The lowest address of a loaded assembly language program -- the first byte loaded. Not necessarily the same as the entry point address (EPA).
LOGICAL	A form of arithmetic which operates with binary "truth" or "false", 1 or 0. AND, OR, NAND, NOR, and EXCLUSIVE OR are all logical operations.
LOOP	A programming construction in which a group of instructions or statements are repeatedly executed.
LOW MEMORY	The memory locations with the lowest addresses. $0000 is the lowest memory location. Also called the "bottom" of memory.
LOMEM	APPLE's zero-page address which identifies the first byte of the available memory which can be used to store BASIC programs and their variables.
LSB/LO ORDER	Least Significant Bit or Least Significant Byte. The 1's bit in a byte or the second pair of hexadecimal digits forming an address. In the address $8030, $30 is the LO order part of the address.
MASTER DISK	A DOS diskette which will boot in an APPLE II of any size memory and take full advantage of it.
MICROSECOND	A millionth of a second. Equivalent to one cycle of the APPLE II central processor. Also written as "Usec".
MONITOR	A machine language program which always resides in the computer and which is the first to receive control when the machine is powered up. The APPLE monitor resides in ROM and allows examination and modification of memory at a byte level.

MSB/HI ORDER — Most Significant Bit or Most Significant Byte. The 128's bit of a byte (the left-most) or the first pair of hexadecimal digits in an address. In the byte value $83, the MSB is on (is a 1).

NULL — Empty, having no length or value. A null string is one which contains no characters. The null control character ($00) produces no effect on a printer (also called an idle).

NIBBLE/NYBBLE — A portion of a byte, usually 4 bits and represented by a single hexadecimal digit. $FE contains two nibbles, $F and $E.

OBJECT CODE — A machine language program in binary form, ready to execute. Object code is the output of an assembler.

OBJECT MODULE — A complete machine language program in object code form, stored as a file on a diskette.

OFFSET — The distance from the beginning of a block of data to a particular byte or field. Offsets are usually given beginning with 0, for the first byte, 1 for the second, etc. Also known as a displacement.

OPCODE — Operation Code. The three letter mnemonic representing a single assembly

for the jump instruction.

OPERATING SYSTEM — A machine language program which manages the memory and peripherals automatically, simplifying the job of the applications programmer.

OR — The logical operation comparing two bits to determine if either of them are 1. 1 OR 1 results in 1 (true), 1 OR 0 results in 1, 0 OR 0 results in 0 (false).

OVERHEAD — The space required by the system, either in memory or on the disk, to manage either. The disk directory and VTOC are part of a diskette's overhead.

PAGE — 256 bytes of memory which share a common high order address byte. Zero page is the first 256 bytes of memory ($0000 through $00FF).

PARALLEL	Opposite of serial. A communication mode which sends all of the bits in a byte at once, each over a separate line or wire.
PARAMETER LIST	An area of storage set aside for communication between a calling program and a subroutine. The parameter list contains input and output variables which will be used by the subroutine.
PARITY	A scheme, similar to checksums but on a bit level rather than a byte level, which allows detection of errors in a single data byte. An extra parity bit is attached to each byte which is a sum of the bits in the byte. Parity is used in expensive memory to detect or correct single bit failures, and when sending data over communications lines to detect noise errors.
PARSE	The process of interpreting character string data, such as a command with keywords.
PATCH	A small change to the object code of an assembly language program. Also called a "zap".
PERIPHERAL	A device which is external to the computer itself, such as a disk drive or a printer. Also called an Input/Output device.
PHYSICAL RECORD	A collection of data corresponding to the smallest unit of storage on a peripheral device. For disks, a physical record is a sector.
POINTER	The address or memory location of a block of data or a single data item. The address "points" to the data.
PROLOGUE	The three bytes at the beginning of a disk field which uniquely identify it from any other data on the track.
PROM	Programmable Read Only Memory. PROMs are usually used on controller cards associated with peripherals to hold the driver program which interfaces the device to applications programs.
PROMPT	An output string which lets the user know that input is expected. A "*" is the prompt character for the APPLE monitor.

PROTECTED DISK	A diskette whose format or content has been modified to prevent its being copied. Most retail software today is distributed on protected disks to prevent theft.
PSEUDO-OPCODE	A special assembly language opcode which does not translate into a machine instruction. A pseudo-opcode instructs the assembler to perform some function, such as skipping a page in an assembly listing or reserving data space in the output object code.
RANDOM ACCESS	Direct access. The capability to rapidly access any single piece of data on a storage medium without having to sequentially read all of its predecessors.
RAM	Random Access Memory. Computer memory which will allow storage and retrieval of values by address.
RECAL	Recalibrate the disk arm so that the read/write head is positioned over track zero. This is done by pulling the arm as far as it will go to the outside of the diskette until it hits a stop, producing a "clacking" sound.
RECORD	A collection of associated data items or fields. One or more records are usually associated with a file. Each record might correspond to an employee, for example.
REGISTER	A named temporary storage location in the central processor itself. The 6502 has 5 registers; the A, X, Y, S, and P registers. Registers are used by an assembly language program to access memory and perform arithmetic.
RELEASE	A version of a distributed piece of software. There have been several releases of DOS.
RELOCATABLE	The attribute of an object module file which contains a machine language program and the information necessary to make it run at any memory location.

RETURN CODE — A numeric value returned from a subroutine, indicating the success or failure of the operation attempted. A return code of zero usually means there were no errors. Any other value indicates the nature of the error, as defined by the design of the subroutine.

ROM — Read Only Memory. Memory which has a permanent value. The APPLE monitor and BASIC interpreters are stored in ROM.

RWTS — Read/Write Track/Sector. A collection of subroutines which allow access to the diskette at a track and sector level. RWTS is part of DOS and may be called by external assembly language programs.

SEARCH — The process of scanning a track for a given sector.

SECTOR — The smallest updatable unit of data on a disk track. One sector on an APPLE DISK II contains 256.data bytes.

SECTOR ADDRESS — A disk field which identifies the sector data field which follows in terms of its volume, track, and sector number.

SECTOR DATA — A disk field which contains the actual sector data in nibbilized form.

SEEK — The process of moving the disk arm to a given track.

SELF-SYNC — Also called "auto-sync" bytes. Special disk bytes which contain more than 8 bits, allowing synchronization of the hardware to byte boundaries when reading.

SEQUENTIAL ACCESS — A mode of data retreival where each byte of data is read in the order in which it was written to the disk.

SERIAL — As opposed to parallel. A communication mode which sends data bits one at a time over a single line or wire.

SHIFT — A logical operation which moves the bits of a byte either left or right one position, moving a 0 into the bit at the other end.

SLAVE DISK	A diskette with a copy of DOS which is not relocatable. The DOS image will always be loaded into the same memory location, regadless of the size of the machine.
SOFT ERROR	A recoverable I/O error. A worn diskette might produce soft errors occasionally.
SOFTWARE	Computer programs and data which can be loaded into RAM memory and executed.
SOURCE CODE	A program in a form which is understandable to humans; in character form as opposed to internal binary machine format. Source assembly code must be processed by an assembler to translate it into machine or "object" code.
SKEWING	The process of interleaving sectors. See INTERLEAVE.
STATE MACHINE	A process (in software or hardware) which defines a unique target state, given an input state and certain conditions. A state machine approach is used in DOS to keep track of its video intercepts and by the hardware on the disk controller card to process disk data.
STROBE	The act of triggering an I/O function by momentarily referencing a special I/O address. Strobing $C030 produces a click on the speaker. Also called "toggling".
SUBROUTINE	A program whose function is required repeatedly during execution, and therefore is called by a main program in several places.
TABLE	A collection of data entries, having similar format, residing in memory. Each entry might contain the name of a program and its address, for example. A "lookup" can be performed on such a table to locate any given program by name.
TOGGLE	The act of triggering an I/O function by momentarily referencing a special I/O address. Toggling $C030 produces a click on the speaker. Also called "strobe".

TOKENS	A method where human recognizable words may be coded to single binary byte values for memory compression and faster processing. BASIC statements are tokenized, where hex codes are assigned to words like IF, PRINT, and END.
TRACK	One complete circular path of magnetic storage on a diskette. There are 35 concentric tracks on an APPLE diskette.
TRANSLATE TABLE	A table of single byte codes which are to replace input codes on a one-for-one basis. A translate table is used to convert from 6 bit codes to disk codes.
T/S LIST	Track/Sector List. A sector which describes the location of a file by listing the track and sector number for each of its data sectors in the order that they are to be read or written.
TTL	Transistor to Transistor Logic. A standard for the interconnection of integrated circuits which also defines the voltages which represent 0's and 1's.
UTILITY	A program which is used to maintain, or assist in the development of, other programs or disk files.
VECTOR	A collection of pointers or JMP instructions at a fixed location in memory which allow access to a relocatable program or data.
VOLUME	An identification for a diskette, disk platter, or cassette, containing one or more files.
VTOC	Volume Table Of Contents. Based upon the IBM OS/VS VTOC. On the APPLE, a sector mapping the free sectors on the diskette and giving the location of the directory.
WARMSTART	A restart of a program which retains, as much as is possible, the work which was in progress at the time. A DOS warmstart retains the BASIC program in memory.
WRITE PROTECTED	A diskette whose write protect notch is covered, preventing the disk drive from writing on it.

ZAP	From the IBM utility program, SUPERZAP. A program which allows updates to a disk at a byte level, using hexadecimal.
ZERO PAGE	The first 256 bytes of memory in a 6502 based machine. Zero page locations have special significance to the central processor, making their management and assignment critical.

INDEX

Order Form

ISBN/PRODUCT NUMBER	QUANTITY	DESCRIPTION	MEDIUM (CASS/DISK)	AMOUNT

SUBTOTAL	
(CA RESIDENTS) SALES TAX	
SHIPPING	
TOTAL	

CHECK # ______________

OR VISA/MASTERCARD # ______________________________ EXPIRES ________

NAME ______________________________

STREET ADDRESS ______________________________

CITY, STATE, POSTAL CODE ______________________________

COUNTRY ______________________________

Prices Subject to Change Without Notice

BAG OF TRICKS 2
A Super Disk Utility by the Authors of Beneath Apple DOS
$49.95

If you find BENEATH APPLE DOS useful, you should also find BAG OF TRICKS 2 an important help in examining and patching up your disks.

BAG OF TRICKS 2 is a package of four machine language subroutines which go far beyond the example programs in Appendix A of this book. User friendly and well documented, this disk utility package is undoubtedly the best one available for the Apple II, especially at the low price of $49.95.

BAG OF TRICKS 2 is designed for 5¼″ floppies, but it also performs many valuable functions for 3½″ floppies, some hard disks, and RAM disks. For example, it will reconstruct ProDOS directories on a ProFile hard disk. All popular operating systems, DOS 3.3, ProDOS, Pascal, and CP/M, are supported. And the programs come on a standard ProDOS disk that is not copy protected.

The four programs and their functions are:

1. TRAX dumps and analyzes a track of data from a 5¼″ diskette. The internal Apple diskette formatting information is displayed and exceptions to standard formats are noted.
2. INIT reformats one or more tracks on a 5¼″ diskette, or copies a whole disk to another disk, even if one or more sectors on the disk are damaged.
3. ZAP allows you to read, display, and change data in a disk sector or block. More than 50 commands are available. Printer support too. Works with 3½″ disks, ProFile, Sider, and RAM disks, as well as 5¼″ diskettes. Files can be accessed by filename.
4. FIXCAT automates the process of recovering a damaged DOS catalog or ProDOS directory. Lost files can be recovered. If your directory is fixable, FIXCAT can fix it!

If you ever had a disk crash, you know what a good disk utility is worth. Beginners will appreciate the "hand holding" tutorials in the complete documentation that comes with BAG OF TRICKS 2. Experienced users will appreciate how fast and easily they can perform analysis and repairs.

BAG OF TRICKS 2 runs on Apple II, II+, IIe, or IIc. 64K and one 5¼″ disk drive are required.

TURN PAGE FOR ORDERING INFORMATION.

Ordering Directly from Quality Software

To order our products directly, mail the order form on this page to Quality Software (at the below address) with your payment—the price of the software (plus sales tax for California residents) *plus* shipping charges.* Your payment can be a check or bank draft made payable to Quality Software in US dollars, or your VISA or MASTERCARD number and expiration date (VISA and MASTERCARD holders may phone in their orders). California residents must add the appropriate sales tax (6 or 6.5%). No CODs will be accepted.

***Shipping Charges**

48 Continental United States (UPS)	$ 2.50
Alaska, Hawaii, Canada, and Mexico (air mail)	$ 5.00
All other countries (insured air mail)	$10.00

Send your orders to:

QS QUALITY SOFTWARE
21601 Marilla Street
Chatsworth, CA 91311
Phone (818) 709-1721